WHAT THEY DIDN'T TEACH YOU IN SEMINARY

Dr. Frank Minirth
Dr. Paul Meier
Dr. Brian Newman
Dr. Richard Meier
Dr. Allen R. Doran
Dr. David Congo

A
JANET
THOMA
BOOK

THOMAS NELSON PUBLISHERS
Nashville

Published in Nashville, Tennessee, by Thomas Nelson, Inc., and distributed in Canada by Lawson Falle, Ltd., Cambridge, Ontario.

Scripture quotations are from THE NEW KING JAMES VERSION. Copyright © 1979, 1980, 1982, Thomas Nelson, Inc., Publishers.

Library of Congress Cataloging-in-Publication Data

What they didn't teach you in seminary / Paul Meier . . . [et al.].
    p.   cm.
   ISBN 0-8407-7708-6
   1. Clergy—Office.   2. Pastoral theology.   I. Meier, Paul D.
BV660.2.W43   1993
253'.2—dc20   92–27058
                                               CIP

Printed in the United States of America.
1 2 3 4 5 6 7 8 9 10 — 97 96 95 94 93

Acknowledgments

The authors are grateful to Kay Strom for her expertise in writing that enabled her to compile this book from their combined writings and information. And we are especially thankful to our families, whose patience and graciousness allowed us the time to fulfill the commitment to this.

Many thanks, also, to Janet Thoma at Thomas Nelson Publishers for her encouragement and wisdom, as well as to her senior staff members, H. Susan Salmon and Laurie Clark, and to the rest of the Nelson staff.

Most of all, we send a heartfelt message to the pastors to whom this project is directed. We offer you our compassion and encouragement along with the contents of this book; for with your influence, many of us came to learn of God's gift of salvation and the importance of developing a personal relationship with Christ. Now it's our turn to give you something.

Contents

*"Mastering Your Mammon" was contributed by Ethan Pope, CFP and founder and president of Financial Foundations For Living, Hattiesburg, MS.

PART FIVE: Leaders, Strong and True

GOD'S FRONT LINE

1

What's a Pastor to Do?

L et me tell you about Rob. A strong soccer player in high school, he was recruited by a small private college with an aggressive athletic program. It was there at college, in a group conducted on campus by a local pastor, that he first heard about the possibility of having a personal relationship with Jesus Christ, the Son of God. And there, during his freshman year, the brash, boisterous jock became a Christian.

There was an immediate and dramatic change in Rob's life. He quickly dropped out of the wild fraternity scene. No longer was he an enthusiastic participant of the uninhibited nights out on the town. Rob was changed.

By nature, Rob was the kind of fellow who would do anything for anyone at any time. If someone's car didn't start in the morning, Rob was the one to offer a ride. If a person needed a loan, Rob was right there ready to help. He went the extra mile for everybody. Not only was he a truly nice guy with a wonderful sense of humor, he was also a hard worker. Little wonder that he was elected student body president in his senior year.

The minister who led Rob to Christ had been a tennis coach at Princeton University before he entered the ministry. Perhaps it was his obvious love for all sports that attracted Rob and his friends into his church, or perhaps it

3

was the pastor's loving concern and true care for the young men. Without a doubt it was due to the minister's influence that Rob decided that he, too, wanted to be a pastor.

After seminary, Rob started a church in a tiny midwestern town. He and his wife, Beverly, rented a little house, and with four other dedicated couples, his pastoral adventure began. The little group met in homes each week, and each week their numbers grew. Before long they decided to build a church, and build is exactly what they did. After constructing the entire building themselves, they carefully added a lovely parsonage for Rob and Beverly.

Beverly was a wonderful Christian woman, an excellent wife and mother, a dedicated high school teacher, and an all-around fun person; but she wasn't much of a housekeeper, and she didn't like to cook. Her poor housekeeping and "package meals" were a constant problem to the congregation. They whispered criticisms and pointed out to each other what they thought a pastor's wife should be and where Beverly fell short. They formed committees to try to think of ways to help Beverly. Women appeared at her door and announced they were there to take care of the kids so that Beverly would have time to "get the house in order."

To make matters worse, members of the congregation popped in unexpectedly and at all hours. Some walked in without so much as an announcing knock. One evening Rob and Beverly had a family of out-of-town friends in for dinner. Beverly had outdone herself—she prepared a turkey with all the trimmings. Suddenly, in the middle of dinner, a woman burst in and said she was having trouble with her adolescent son. "You need to come and talk to him," she told Rob. No one else would do. No other time would work. And, oh yes, Beverly must come along to offer her husband support. Before they knew what happened, Rob and Beverly's guests found themselves sitting at the table before an unfinished dinner, surrounded by kids, with no host or hostess.

Without a doubt, the little church loved their pastor. They loved him so much they couldn't be without him. They insisted he be on call, every day, all the time, always ready to solve any problem.

Although Rob had many strengths, he was not what you would call a charismatic person. He provided his congregation with good, sound biblical teaching, but more than a few members were known to have drifted off to sleep during his sermons. Yet the church continued to grow. Rob was a good, steadfast pastor who had a sincere heart for his flock.

After being at the church for eight years, Rob started to meet weekly with a psychologist friend. There were problems, he knew that, and he could feel the pressures mounting. His ministry had no boundaries. Church members came and went at will with little consideration for his family's need for privacy. People constantly turned to him for counseling, even though he wasn't really trained as a counselor. When he looked around at his little flock, what he saw was evidence of the same sins that were rampant outside the church walls, and that bothered him terribly.

Shortly after his fifteenth anniversary at the church, Rob announced he was leaving the ministry. It had been his one and only church, and he had put more than his heart into it—he had given it his life. As for the congregation, they were crushed. They begged him to stay. He smiled and thanked them for their love and told them he truly cared for them, but he insisted he had to go. When Rob left the church, he left the ministry.

The church Rob had started from nothing had developed into a moderate-sized, ever-growing congregation. In the fifteen years he served as their pastor, there was never so much as a hint of a split. By most any assessment, Rob had had a successful ministry. He had done his job well. So what happened?

Long-Term Stress, Eventual Burnout

You ministers are vitally important to our society. You are God's major front line. We cannot afford to discourage or disillusion you. We dare not stand by and watch the stresses and pressures to which you are subjected build to where they cause you to burn out. You are far too important to us.

Roy Oswald, a senior consultant of The Alban Institute—a nondenominational organization based in Washington, D.C., that offers help for churches and synagogues across the nation—makes a conservative estimate that 17 percent of the clergy members with whom he has worked are suffering from long-term stress or burnout.[1] What this emphasizes is something you already know— ministers are human.

Like every one of us, you have questions you need answered, concerns you need addressed, and problems for which you need counsel. Not only must you carry your own personal pressures, but you are expected to bear our problems as well. And what do you get for your labors? A lot of bad press. That can't help but add to your stress level. And then there is the rest of the Christian community and their expectations. Everyone's eyes are on you, insisting that you and your family always and without exception walk the Christian walk. You are expected to work without break or complaint and to be satisfied with little more than a token salary.

Pastor, we don't want it to be this way. Whatever your problems and stresses, you have a right—no, a responsibility—to seek relief. We want you to know that many people are ready and waiting to come alongside you, people who are saying, "Hey, we understand. We don't want to lose you, and we don't want your ministry to suffer. We care about you and appreciate what you're doing, and we want to help."

A couple of years ago, a pastor came to us suffering from long-standing depression. "I've been seeing psychiatrists for years now," he said. "They have told me many things and given me a good deal of advice, but no one ever told me I could get better."

"No one?" Dr. Minirth asked incredulously. "Why, that's ridiculous. Of course you can get better." He then reminded that minister of the words of the apostle Paul: "I can do all things through Christ who strengthens me" (Phil. 4:13). And he added, "That includes getting over this depression. You *can* overcome this."

The pastor's eyes grew bright. He looked straight at Dr. Minirth and said, "Do you *really* think I can?"

"I'm certain of it!" Dr. Minirth replied. Then he spent a good deal of time talking with the man and reassuring him. He also put him on a mild antidepressant.

A couple of days later the minister strode into the office looking like a new man. "I feel better than I've felt in twenty years!" he told us, and his big smile and hearty handshake all-around convinced us of what he said.

What had made the difference? It couldn't possibly have been the antidepressant, because it takes such medication two or three weeks to work. No, what made the difference was hope. Someone cared about him. Someone was confident he could be all right. Someone didn't blame him for how he felt.

For a minister to go through life feeling bad about himself, thinking negative thoughts, suffering in silence, burning out, and feeling more and more hopeless is a terrible waste. If the problem is medical—which in the case of depression it sometimes is—the sufferer needs treatment from a medical doctor. If it is spiritual, he needs someone to assist him toward spiritual renewal, just as he so patiently and faithfully helps so many others along. If it is psychological, he needs psychological guidance and rest and healing in exactly the same way the rest of us do. And he owes no one an explanation or an apology He is human like the rest of us.

You are so very important to the body of Christ. We need you healthy and strong. And we want you to know there is help and relief for whatever stresses and pressures are holding you back from soaring to your potential.

The Magnifying Mirror for Society

When troubles and anxieties rise in society, people bring their pressures and frustrations with them to church. They expect comfort and help from thier pastor. But what's a pastor to do? How can he sufficiently meet the diverse and often desperate needs of everyone?

What happens is that ministers try frantically to be all things to all people. But as many of you know, however much you do, it's not enough. There just aren't enough solutions to go around. When the day comes to an end and it's time to go home, you can't quit because there is always someone else still in need.

Today society's problems are many: unemployment, financial despair, homelessness, addictions of all kinds, abuse, broken families and broken people, frustration, loneliness, discouragement, hopelessness. And all those problems are piled onto the backs of you pastors who really care and truly want to make a difference.

We hear about the publicized scandals involving overstressed clergy. It's disheartening, yet it is undeniably true that pressures and stresses do take their toll. Sometimes it is in the form of sexual misconduct, sometimes alcoholism or drug abuse, other times overeating or any one of various other addictions. It can result in depression, anxiety, even health threats such as ulcers and heart attacks. For instance, in 1990, the Southern Baptist Convention reported that, after maternity benefits, the largest portion of the $64.2 million paid to pastors in medical claims during the previous year was for stress-related illness.[2]

Most pastors do extremely well at juggling the pressures thrust upon them. At times some do get into serious trouble and need more help than they can get from a book. But all pastors, even the best, hurt at times. And it is during these times that the principles and suggestions and exercises within this book can guide you toward greater health and wholeness.

Care for Yourself

Members of the prestigious Wieuca Road Baptist Church of Atlanta were shocked when their longtime pastor told them he was resigning because the stress of his job was too much for him. "Unless I quit now," Dr. William Self told them, "my obituary will read, 'Bill Self today sank like a rock—beat up, burned out, angry, and depressed, no good to himself, no good to the people he loved.'"

Dr. Self was no amateur in the ministry. The fifty-eight-year-old pastor had been tirelessly serving the Lord for more than a quarter of a century. His problem? He put it this way: "I did not have a crisis of faith, but of emotion and energy. It's almost impossible for leaders of a congregation to accept that their pastor needs pastoring." If he were to survive, he decided, he would have to stop waiting for others to take care of him. He would have to start taking care of himself.[3]

You are trained to help others. You are accustomed to meeting the needs of those around you. But somehow it's difficult for most pastors to see that it's all right—in fact, that it is *vital*—to tend to their own needs as well. Every pastor needs to conduct some self-counseling and self-evaluation when he undergoes the stresses and realities his life brings him.

Dr. Self, now an Atlanta business executive, is in demand as a "minister to ministers." "Pastors are still the front line in caring for people," he insists. "But they have a longing for people to turn around and care for them, too. Well, that's just not the reality of church life. So I tell young men and women in the ministry to create a pattern of taking care of themselves. Nobody else is going to do it."[4]

How well are you doing at taking care of yourself? The following Life-style Balance Assessment[5] will give you an idea of where you are balanced, where you are moving toward balance, where you are moving away from balance, and where you may be out of control.

It is our sincere hope and prayer that *What They Didn't Teach You in Seminary* will assist you in finding the right balance in your life. Some of us have traveled this journey of looking for balance in the pastorate. Richard Meier was a pastor for twenty-three years before he joined his brother, Paul Meier, as a counselor at the Minirth-Meier Clinic in Dallas. Dr. David Congo served for seven years as a pastor before getting his Ph.D. in clinical psychology and beginning practice with the Minirth-Meier-Stoop Clinic in California. Dr. Brian Newman served for a year and a half as a pastor of a church while studying for his master's in counseling. With degress in medicine and theology, Dr. Frank

Life-style Balance Assessment

Goal: A Balanced life-style.

Life-Style	Out of Control	Moving away from Balance	Moving toward Balance	Balanced
1. I take time for myself.				
2. I allow for periods of relaxation.				
3. When I am tired I rest.				
4. I develop new interests and hobbies.				
5. I take time for my appearance.				
6. I take time for meditation, devotions, and prayer.				
7. I maintain healthy eating habits.				
8. I maintain a healthy weight.				
9. I maintain and develop my sense of humor.				
10. I take time to plan.				
11. I take time for a date night.				

Life-Style	Out of Control	Moving away from Balance	Moving toward Balance	Balanced
12. I am self-aware.				
13. I am physically healthy.				
14. I take time to work on my marriage.				
15. I spend time with my children.				
16. I maintain old relationships.				
17. I take time to develop new relationships.				
18. I have a support group.				
19. I deal with interpersonal conflict.				
20. Forgiving is a high priority.				
21. I make my deadlines.				
22. I take time for my ministry.				
23. Facing my anger is a high priority.				
24. I need others' approval.				

Life-Style	Out of Control	Moving away from Balance	Moving toward Balance	Balanced
25. I live in the present rather than in the past.				
26. I acknowledge my mistakes and see them as necessary for my growth.				
27. I have a healthy sex life.				
28. I take one day off a week.				
29. I feel as if I am in control of my time.				
30. I feel as if I'm adapting to the changes brought on by my age.				
31. I feel like I'm adapting to those unexpected life crises.				
32. I can assertively express my needs and beliefs.				
33. I am learning to face my fears.				
34. I feel I am a person of worth and value.				
35. I am in control of my finances.				
36. I feel spiritually nourished by my relationship with God.				

Minirth and Dr. Paul Meier, co-founders of the Minirth-Meier Clinic, have taught pastoral counseling in seminaries. Dr. Allen Doran has used his degrees in theology and psychiatry in counseling with hundreds of pastors across the country.

This book is intended to be a comprehensive, personal handbook that can assist you in dealing with the realities of your life as a pastor. Help and hope and guidance on where and how to find answers—that's what this book is all about.

We will begin with the realities of your day-to-day life—we call it living in a stained-glass pressure cooker. Those issues include the pressures you deal with day in, day out—both the internal and the external, the financial and those you encounter in the counseling room. Then we will consider those relationships that cement your life in place—relationships with your spouse and children, and relationships within the church body. From there we will look at your role as a shepherd: What is expected of you? How can you avoid the morals morass that has engulfed too many of your co-workers? And how will you care for yourself? In the last section, we will talk about your personal wholeness and your value to the body of Christ.

Now let's begin at the beginning, with the way it is.

STAINED-GLASS PRESSURE COOKER

2

The Way It Is

An oak plaque hanging in a minister's office reads: "Serving God may not pay much, but the rewards are out of this world." Cleverly written words, but a somewhat disturbing truth. Certainly, ministry brings its rewards, even in this world. Yet there are also some very difficult realities with which pastors have to deal in the here and now.

Let's look at some of the realities you are likely facing in your own ministry.

Reality #1: You Are a Highly Visible, Public Person

By definition, ministers work with people. That's what ministering is all about.

"When we were in the pastorate, we really loved the people," says Dick Meier. "But come my day off, Lorraine and I wanted to get out of town. We needed privacy and time alone."

But even getting away isn't always enough.

"Some of the places we would go to get away, we'd still run into people," Dick recalls. "We'd be sitting in a little place having a hot dog and talking, and someone would tap us on the shoulder and say, 'Hi! Got a minute?' Then the person would pull up a chair and join us."

When you're a public person, it's hard to get time alone. But pressures also touch the families of public people.

We got a note from a pastor's wife saying that their church's youth leader expects more out of her teenage son than other kids in the youth group just because he's a pastor's kid. In this man's view, the pastor's son shouldn't be allowed to experience the temptations, the mistakes, and the failures other young people go through. The boy was expected to be ultraspiritual and mature at all times. After all, he was the pastor's son. "When he isn't perfect," the frustrated mother wrote, "the youth leader makes a big deal of it to him, then he makes a point of reporting to us."

The effects of being highly visible are even more evident in the life of the pastor's wife. "I was criticized because I didn't give my husband good eye contact when he was preaching," said one wife. "I was informed that if I looked bored, people would think we were having problems."

While there is a negative side to being highly visible, there is also a positive side. Ministers have a definite place of influence that reaches beyond the confines of their own congregation. You, Pastor, are in a position to make a real difference in the lives of people around you. But there is a catch: to make a difference you must be open and real enough to let the people around you see that you are human. This gives them permission to be human too. Are you willing to let others see your struggles, your hurts, your failures? Watching you live can give them the strength to live their own lives with a little more grace.

High visibility comes with the territory. If your tendency is to look for a place to hide, try to move toward accepting both the good and the bad of this reality.

You may be saying to yourself, "Well, that's all well and good if I do well. But what if I blow it?" It's true that your errors, too, are highly visible. The answer? One retired minister, a man with great wisdom and a wonderful sense of humor, lives by this rule: "If I lay an egg, I want to write my name on it and hold it up to the congregation. I want to let them see it before they find out about it on their own." Pretty good advice. The best defense is offense. Take the wind out of your mistake before others can snatch it up and throw it back in your face.

You *are* a person in a public, highly visible position. But it can be a pretty good place to be.

Reality #2: You Face the Stress of Forced Creativity

Having to come up with something new, something exciting, something that will inspire and move your congregation to action week after week, month after month, and year after year is a real point of stress for most pastors. Perhaps it's always been tough, but today it's a monumental challenge. There is such an explosion of possibilities in the media, on television, in books, tapes, and videos that many a pastor wonders how he can manage to glean from Scripture something new and relevant and present it to people who are so used to being entertained. How does he put forth the biblical message so that it touches people where they live?

And success merely compounds the pressure. If you do well for a period of time, it just serves to heighten the congregation's expectations. A good job this week leaves everyone expecting at least as good a presentation—preferably a better one—next week.

In a poll conducted by *Christianity Today* and the Gallup organization, a cross section of clergy were asked what they considered the most important activities of pastoral ministry. Fifty-six percent of those responding singled out preaching. Yet this doesn't necessarily mean they feel their preaching is effective. When they were asked "What programs in your church are especially successful?" less than 10 percent mentioned preaching.[1]

What can you do to keep your sermons fresh and alive? The good news is that the very same media advances that have informed, educated, and entertained your congregation can also be used to your advantage. Many books have been written to help you, including volumes containing examples and anecdotes, sermon outlines, and relevant texts. There are also magazines to guide you, as well as videos and tapes.[2] Don't hesitate to make use of these resources.

Let your people help you too. From time to time, pass out a survey sheet to the congregation asking them to list their top five concerns, difficulties, needs, or struggles. By doing this, you can keep in touch with their felt needs and address those needs with the Scriptures.

Others in the ministry can also provide you with many good suggestions. For instance, in order to keep his messages relevant, one pastor goes to the public library every week and spends half an hour looking at the article titles on the new magazines. When he sees a topic covered in four separate periodicals, he knows he has found a subject whose relevancy is worth considering. Look through the material available and see what you might incorporate into your own preaching.

Reality #3: Not Everyone Will Like You and Your Family

Many ministers are dearly loved by their congregations. Many are greatly respected in their communities. Many have wives and children who are adored. But the pastor who is liked by everyone doesn't exist. No matter who you are and how hard you try, you are not going to be universally loved and accepted and neither is your family.

Actually, this is not surprising. None of us can be all things to all people. Whatever we are, however we do things, someone will want it different. No matter how strong your strengths and how diligent your work, you are going to get criticism from one side or the other. That's how it is when you're working with people.

Because we all want to be liked, it hurts when we are criticized and seen as unacceptable. "I remember when I was fresh out of seminary, just starting out in my first church," says Dave Congo. "I was helping in the services, and my wife, Jan, was singing in the choir. We were so short of money, I only had one wearable suit. After we had been at the church about six weeks, one Sunday morning a woman leaned over to Jan in the choir loft and whispered, 'Can't your husband wear another suit?' Jan wanted to whisper back, 'Well, if you'd pay him a little more, he could!' Fortunately, she practiced self-control and kept quiet."

You're going to get criticism, and most often you won't get the satisfaction of an apology. It will be especially hard to deal with when you feel the person has not earned the right to criticize you. Perhaps she doesn't even know you. Maybe he hasn't made an effort to spend any time with you. It may be that the critical person made a snap decision based on something very superficial.

A distraught woman came to us for help. Her minister husband, she told us, had been a perfectionist, locked into real "all or nothing" thinking. To him, his ministry was total success or total failure. When one of his board members sent him a scathingly critical letter, he laid the letter out on his desk and shot himself in the head. It was just one complaint, but to him it was too devastating to bear.

The reality of criticism and rejection can indeed be devastating, even if it is exaggerated in the mind of the minister. One pastor came to Dave Congo saying he was frighteningly close to burning out. When Dave asked if he received affirmation from his congregation he said, "Yes, as a matter of fact I do." He pulled out a manila envelope. "When I get encouraging notes I stick them in here. Then, when I get discouraged, I can pull some out and they encourage me to keep on going."

"Why don't you read me a few?" Dave asked.

The man took out half a dozen notes and read them out loud. Every one of the comments was targeted at something the pastor had done: "Last week the sermon really touched me," "Thank you for starting the new junior high youth group. Our kids are real excited," "Thank you for calling on my mother in the hospital. It meant a lot to her. She talked about it for the rest of the week."

Then Dave asked him if he ever got criticism. (A loaded question for a pastor!) "Of course I do," he said. "Recently I've gotten some pretty strong criticism."

Dave asked him for a few examples.

"Just last week I got something that sounds like it was sent by a character assassin. The writer was really attacking me. It wasn't about something I'd done, not like I'd handled a meeting wrong or didn't start the program they wanted. It said things like, 'You're an insensitive pastor. You're uncaring. You're on a real ego trip.'"

Hear the difference? The affirmation this pastor received focused on his performance, whereas the criticism focused on him as a person. The difference between the two is a crucial component that proves devastating to pastors—and to many of the rest of us as well. The good news is that you can help people in your congregation switch from this damaging focus. Point out the importance of affirming other people for who they are. Teach the importance of saying such things as: "You are a caring person. You show it in the way you . . . ," "Thank you for . . . ," "What you did for me tells me so much about who you are. I love that about you." Demonstrate this by affirming others from the pulpit. If your congregation learns to affirm each other, they will be able to affirm you as well.

The reality that not everyone will like you is especially hard for those pastors who have a deep need for approval and love. For some of us, a love deficit from the past makes us more vulnerable. This is complicated by the fact that a minister's job is a conditional love situation. He is reassessed every Sunday. Like a football coach, his job is on the line with every game. At least, that's how many pastors feel. We have counseled pastors who are devastated by how quickly a church or church board members can turn on them. All goes well for several years, then some issue comes up and the people do a complete flip-flop. So much positive can be wiped out so quickly over such amazingly trivial matters. What is left are pastors who are depressed and distressed and discouraged.

"I remember reading that the average person, in any given situation, will be liked by 20 percent of the people no matter what they do," says Dick Meier. "Sixty percent will reserve judgment until they see what they will get from you. You're not going to get the other 20 percent to like you regardless of what you do or say. Either you're too young or too old, too loud or too soft, too much of a teacher or too much of a counselor. I decided to look at those statistics as pretty encouraging. If only about 10 percent of the people in my church didn't like me, I must be above average!"

Most ministers don't see it that way. They want 99 percent of the people to like them. When it doesn't happen, they ask, "What's wrong with me? What did I do wrong? I must be a failure!"

Dick Meier contributed this paraphrase of 1 Corinthians 4:3–4: "I care very little if I am judged by you. . . . I do not even judge myself (I do not stand around all day introspecting). My conscience is clear. It is the Lord who judges me." In his writing, the apostle Paul assures us that it's a very small thing to be judged by others. Are you looking at people's judgment as a very big thing? If so, first examine yourself to be sure that your conscience is clear—that you are following God in the light He has given you. If you're confident that this is so, work toward developing in yourself a healthy attitude of concerned detachment.

Reality #4: Your Income May Be Lower Than That of Many of Your Church Members

This is not always true; but for many pastors, the lack of a fair salary is a definite point of stress in their lives. Given the hours required of a minister, the pressures of the pastorate, and the level of education required of members of the clergy, the pay offered often seems too low.

Part of the problem is that too many Christians see the privilege of serving God as its own reward. Others see the pastor's salary as yet another area open for criticism. If he and his family wear nice clothes, for instance, people complain that "we're paying the pastor too much." Yet if he and his family dress too poorly, the people feel ashamed of them.

Fortunately, more and more churches today are acknowledging the problem of ministers' low pay and are coming up with a formula to govern the salaries they offer. One church's rule of thumb is that its pastor's pay will be the average pay of the members of the board. Others base it on an average income of the church members.

If too low a salary is a problem for you, perhaps it is time you shared your needs and concerns with the chairman of the church board or another trusted board member. Without accusing or complaining, let him know the financial needs of your family. Hard to do, you say? You can't bring yourself to broach such a sensitive subject? It might help to talk the matter over with other pastors in your area and find out how they are communicating with their board members on the subject of finances. Ask them for specific suggestions. (One minister suggested asking the board chairman to survey three or four churches of a size similar to theirs to find a salary range.)

If you are an assertive person, this may not be too difficult for you. But if you are one who is reluctant to make waves, you will likely have to prepare more thoroughly. Some pastors feel: *I shouldn't have to say anything to the church about pay. They should know I need more. If they really cared about me, they would give me a raise. If I bring it up, they will probably think I'm selfish and too materialistic.* It isn't fair to expect the church members to read your mind or to intuitively know your needs. It is your responsibility to speak up.

If you are doing your best to meet the needs of your congregation, and if you are faithful in teaching them from the Word of God, you are worthy of your hire. You deserve to be compensated for your labors. Pray about it, talk it over with your wife, then go to a board member and share your concerns. You may be pleasantly surprised at the reception you'll get.

Reality #5: You Have to Live Up to Tough Expectations

Everyone, it seems, wants to perch pastors high up on a pedestal, then watch closely to see that they maintain their precarious position. Too many people expect a minister to be a substitute for God. What person can possibly meet such lofty expectations? The answer is simple: no one. We are just human, every one of us. The stress of struggling to meet super human expectations exacts a terrible toll on many ministers.

To make matters worse, high expectations spill over onto the pastor's entire family. "We had been at our first pastorate for a only few hours," Dave Congo recalls. "Our furniture had just been delivered when a woman came to the door and introduced herself as a member of our new congregation. Her first question to my wife was, 'Are you going to work outside the home?' As a matter of fact, Jan had just finished her master's degree in education and was hoping to do some college teaching.

"Before I could answer our visitor, she turned to Jan and informed her that the previous pastor's wife hadn't been employed, and that she was a 'dear, dear person.' One of her most significant ministries in the church, we were told, was that she used to care for children whose mothers needed a baby-sitter. 'I have three children,' she told Jan, 'and I'm really hoping you'll be available to watch them for me.' The woman was most upset and disappointed when Jan declined."

Reality #6: You Have Expectations of Your Church

As a pastor, you will also have to deal with your own expectations for your church. In general, the lower you keep your expectations, the happier you will be. "The first church I pastored treated me royally," Dick Meier recalls. "Every year they gave our family a nice Christmas bonus."

When Dick moved to a new church, he packed along expectations from that first church experience. In one of his earlier years at the church, he went so far as to share with the chairman of the deacons that it might be a good growing experience for the church to express their appreciation and love by giving an appropriate Christmas bonus to the pastor and staff. Not having had any experience in organizing such a strategy, the chairman just went to a few of the deacons and leaders, taking up a love gift from them rather than from the entire church. "With a thousand members in the church, I expected about a thousand dollars," Dick says. "When I opened the envelope presented to me and took out the forty dollars, I was convinced the people didn't love me. The fact was, my expectations were just too high. Later, that church gave most generously."

The trouble with expectations is that if they aren't met, people tend to become angry or upset—not by what happened, but because "he broke my rules!"

Certainly, some expectations are realistic and fair. But even these should be thoroughly understood by both parties. When a pastor comes into a new church, it's very important that the church present him with a written job description that clearly defines expectations. That way he can decide whether or not he and the church are a compatible fit. It will give both sides a chance to separate their realistic expectations from their unrealistic ones.

Happiness and gratitude go together. And the opposite of gratitude is expectations. Gratitude says, "Thank you so much. You did more than I imagined." Expectations say, "You owe me. I thought you'd do this, and you didn't." The more expectations we have, and the more unrealistic they are, the more likely we are to be disappointed, disillusioned, and frustrated.

Do you expect members of your congregation to be eager to attend every service you conduct? Have you set a rate at which you expect your church membership to grow? How about the growth of the parishioners themselves? Do you expect them to be ready to accept the responsibilities you have in mind for them? Are you counting on them to move from spectators to active participants?

Every one of these is a noble goal. Every one is a trait you would do well to encourage in your congregation. Yet in our busy world, it is unrealistic to expect that you will see these things take place in your congregation as a whole. There are a lot of valid reasons why many good and faithful people won't live up to such expectations. We're not suggesting you give up your goals for your congregation. By all means work toward the best and highest for them. But while you are working and encouraging, be flexible and have some options. For instance, certainly work toward gathering together a complete team of Sunday school teachers. But have a plan B in mind too. If you don't get enough qualified teachers, you might combine classes.

"I know all about a pastor's expectations," says Dick Meier. "I started out in the ministry expecting everyone to love every sermon I preached. I expected to see constant results of my ministry. Claiming Acts 2:47 as my verse, I expected to see people saved every day. I had been told that for a church to be a true New Testament church at least seven people a week should come to the Lord. I took that mandate so seriously that for a while I actually kept a log, writing down names. In time, I decided I would settle for just one new convert a week. During the weeks when someone accepted Christ under my ministry, I considered myself a success. The other weeks, I was convinced I was a failure.

"It took a long time for me to finally realize I'm not responsible for how other people respond. That's a terribly unrealistic expectation for a minister to place on himself. My only responsibility was to be faithful in my ministry."

If you live as God wants you to live, you have a unique opportunity to show others that it truly *is* possible to have a happy home and a satisfying life while serving God. You can demonstrate by example what you preach from the pulpit. First Peter 5 tells us that pastors are to be examples, not bosses or slave drivers. Teaching by example can be a wonderfully successful and satisfying part of your job.

Reality #7: You Have an Open-Ended Job

If you build a cabin, as you work you can take pleasure from watching it take shape. The floors go in, the walls go up, the roof goes on. You paint it and varnish the door, put the doorknobs on, then step back and say, "Wow!" Your project is finished, and you can begin to enjoy it. But that's not how it is with the ministry. Because your building is never finished, you must be able to enjoy your work without that satisfaction of a closure.

For instance, you don't punch a time clock. You don't have weekends free to get away with your family. When people have a problem—any problem—they call you. Whenever a person finds a particular project important, it is expected to be equally important to you, and often your cooperation and help are expected too. Pastoring is an open-ended job. It is never finished. There's always more to be done.

Because of this open-endedness, a pastor needs to carefully organize his time to provide free time for himself, his spouse, and his family—a time to "de-role" and be off duty and relax. He needs to guard his day off with sincere determination. Even if he's the only pastor in the church, he can arrange to have someone on call for emergencies—such as one of the deacons or elders.

Besides Dick's normal day off when he and Lorraine would do things together, some Saturday mornings were times for fun and fellowship with friends. "Lorraine and I and several other couples in the church owned motorcycles," he says. "Frequently, on Saturday mornings we would meet in the K-Mart parking lot, kick each other's tires, check out each other's equipment, and talk about our bikes. I was just one of the bunch, and it felt so good. We'd hop on our bikes and ride somewhere and have breakfast, laughing and enjoying ourselves over our waffles. It was great fun being one of 'Heaven's Angels,' as we called ourselves."

Life in the ministry is going to be busy, but it doesn't have to be a rat race. A strong pastor should teach his congregation the value of priorities, and to do this effectively he must set priorities for himself. What are the proper priorities for a minister? They are the same as for any other godly man.

Priority #1: God

To keep this priority at the top of your list, it may help to start every day with a short time of spiritual inspiration.

Priority #2: Your Spouse

You can't give your wife a high priority unless you take time to know her. Says Dick, "Lorraine and I have found that we need an average of twenty to thirty minutes a night just to gab and catch up on each other's daily activities and interests. But three times a week we take a two-mile walk, and we use this opportunity to do deeper probing. We ask each other such questions as: 'Is there any need in your life I should be aware of? Any concerns? How can I be a better husband (or wife) to you?' Personal probing is like an insurance policy. Rather than waiting for problems to surface, you head them off while they're still small."

Priority #3: Your Children

Dick suggests that the way to get to know your children better is to periodically spend time with each of them alone. Go places and do things. Laugh and enjoy your time together. This will help keep the bridges of communication open so that personal needs and feelings can come to the surface. An added bonus: these times have a way of contributing to your children's sense of self-worth because each one feels uniquely important.

This time can also become a time for indirect teaching of life situations. Dick taught his daughter how to order when she was out with a boy. "Maybe he just has $1.50 in his pocket," he'd tell her, "so follow his lead. Say, 'I don't know what I want. What do you want?' If he says, 'Oh, I just feel like a glass of water and a toothpick' (a pine float!), you can say, 'That sounds good to me too.'"

By your example, teach fathers in your congregation the importance of putting a high priority on fathering.

Priority #4: Other People

Other people are important, but they are the fourth priority. This includes your church, your social activities, and your various involvements.

Priority #5: *Yourself*

Too often ministers don't include themselves on their lists of priorities. It may seem selfless and spiritual to neglect yourself, but it's actually a mistake that can lead to still more stress and eventually to burnout. Carve out time for yourself. For Dick Meier it was riding his motorcycle and flying a private plane. For you it may be playing tennis or going fishing for the day or shopping for antiques.

Usually fitting all five priorities into your week is no problem. The trick is to keep them in balance. If something pushes ahead of the priority above it, you need to pull back and do some reassessment. In an open-ended job like yours, you'll find that keeping your priorities straight will help you achieve good balance in your life.

Reality #8: Crises Never Come at Convenient Times

You are probably well acquainted with this scenario: Your family is just sitting down to dinner when you are interrupted by a phone call. There is a crisis, and you are needed—now!

Crises are never convenient, yet dealing with them is a part of any pastor's life. While this is an area you won't be able to completely change, there are things you can do to help lessen the pressure on yourself.

First, responding to crises is part of the church's call, but ministers should not have to do it alone. You should not consider yourself the only one who can respond to a need. If you are involved in a larger church, you may be able to arrange for a rotation of pastors on call. Also, more and more churches are enlisting laypeople to serve as a crisis team. In one Southern California church such a team is headed by a psychologist who conducts a six-week training program for team members, many of whom have themselves experienced crises and so are especially effective in dealing with those who are hurting.

Next, it is important to set boundaries. What if someone calls and says, "I know this is your day off, but my mother is sick. Would you please go to the hospital and see her? The visit will mean much more coming from you"? It's awfully hard to say no to a worried family member. That's why it is important to set boundaries and then to alert your congregation ahead of time of where those boundaries are. Let people know that there are channels through which they must go. If you are truly needed, you will be notified by the one in charge. But if others try to call you, they will be disappointed because you will not be available. The boundaries you set can involve specific hours, certain days, times of vacation, whatever you need to keep your personal life under control.

Further, enlist the help of your church body. Boundaries mean little if the congregation doesn't accept and respect them. Certainly, it is appropriate to begin by approaching the board members with your need for boundaries, giving them the particulars of what you have in mind. The board can assist you in communicating the boundaries to the congregation by telling them: "We want our pastor to be as effective as possible, and we want to be behind him and to support him to that end. But this means he is not always going to be immediately available. If you call between eight and ten in the morning, you won't get through to him. It's not that you're not important to him, it's just that he needs that uninterrupted study time. Thursdays are his days off. Whether he is at home or not, please respect this time and contact the church with any problems rather than calling him." In the end, it is up to you to kindly but firmly protect your boundaries.

Reality #9: Pastors Aren't Always Held in High Esteem

Not too many years ago ministers, by virtue of their position, were highly respected members of the community— pillars of society. They gave invocations, spoke at public school programs, dedicated new buildings. Today, however, few schools have baccalaureate services. There is even less call for public invocations. Things are different now. For one thing, not nearly as many people go to church anymore. They pride themselves on being educated members of a society that depends on science and technology rather than God. Furthermore, all the negative publicity surrounding "fallen" pastors and the scandals involving television evangelists has cast a shadow over the clergy nationwide.

The important thing is not to seek the esteem of society, which at best is a fleeting thing. What's important is your standing before God. He is the One who sees your motives and judges you lovingly and compassionately. And it is from God that you can derive your own positive self-image.

Reality #10: You May Face Little Job Security

In the area of job security, a great deal of variation exists among denominations. Some ministers are in extremely secure positions. Others are literally at the mercy of the board. A minister might say something that will get an influential member of the congregation up in arms, a congregational meeting will be called, and the minister's resignation demanded almost before he knows what is happening.

When a pastor can be so easily set aside, how can it help but affect what he says from the pulpit? How can it help but affect the stand he is willing to take on social issues? How can it help but affect any conviction where there is the likelihood of opposition?

Job security may or may not be a factor for you. Either way, it is important that you understand just what your position is. Just how secure is your job? What is the procedure for your leaving the church or for being let go? This is a matter both you and the church should understand from the start.

Reality #11: You and Your Family Walk a Tightrope Between Connectedness and Independence

There needs to be a close connection between a pastor and his congregation. He must be close enough to touch people's lives. But a degree of separation is also crucial. Both the minister and his family need identities apart from the church, lest they feel the church is their entire life. The question is: Where should the line between connectedness and independence be drawn?

Finding the right balance is no small challenge, but it is something toward which every minister should continually strive. "Our first home was across the street from church," Dick Meier says. "It was great because we were right in the hub of church life. But it was also awfully hard. People were constantly dropping by. I didn't dare wear my comfortable old T-shirt with the hole under the arm and my faded blue jeans lest someone be offended. We had no privacy. At our next church we lived fourteen miles away. We had to sacrifice the convenience of being right across the street, but the benefits to our family life were well worth it."

Finding your way on the tightrope will surely involve some give and take, and a healthy dose of wise compromise as well.

Hard realities are a part of a pastor's life, but then so are the life-changing benefits. And the end result is that pastors have an enormous amount to offer their congregations, their communities, and the world.

3

Stresses—External and Internal

It was almost midnight on Christmas Eve when Keith Richardson finally arrived home. December had been a hard month, but then, isn't that to be expected for a music minister? When Keith had taken the job five years earlier the church was small; but it had grown rapidly and so had his responsibilities. Now, besides the sanctuary choir, he conducted two youth choirs, several small ensembles, a church orchestra, and he oversaw the children's choirs and all the music for the three weekly worship services. No small responsibility, especially in a month packed with extra rehearsals for all the choirs and small groups, and all the other special Christmas music besides.

Now the last of Keith's four Christmas Eve performances was over. He longed to sink into bed, but he still had the Christmas bicycles to assemble for his twin sons.

As Keith tightened the last screws of the first bike, his wife, Marilyn, put the final gifts under the tree and gathered up the Christmas wrappings and ribbons.

"If you don't need any help, I'm going to bed," Marilyn said. "It's been a long day."

Keith assured her he had everything under control. "The second bike will be a snap," he said. "I'll be in bed within half an hour." Marilyn was not yet asleep when she was startled by the strange sound coming from the living room. It wasn't talking exactly, not crying either. She got up to investigate.

What Marilyn Richardson found in the early hours of that Christmas morning was her husband curled up on the living room floor, sobbing and babbling incoherently. Desperate and terrified, she telephoned us for help.

After two nights of medication and rest in the hospital, we began to work with Keith on the stress factors that had caused him to shut down so completely. Yes, Christmas had been hard, and yes, he was exhausted; but there was a lot more going on beneath the surface. As the second in command after the senior pastor, a lot of responsibility fell to Keith. Whenever there was a problem, or when an interpersonal issue came up on the staff, it inevitably landed in Keith's lap. At that time he was especially struggling with a staff decision to let one of the secretaries go. The decision had been made in November, but it was decided she shouldn't be notified until after Christmas.

"I'm the one who has to tell her she's fired," Keith said miserably. "And it's not even my problem. I like her. I want her to stay."

The woman was not only Keith's secretary, she also led two of his children's choirs. "Not only do I have to do the dirty work, but I'll be out a secretary and a good choir director to boot," he lamented.

There were other stresses as well. For instance, Keith and Marilyn had been trying and trying to scrape together the money to buy a house. "That little apartment is just too small for us and our three children," Keith said wearily. "But however hard we try, we just can't qualify for any financing."

Keith's problems were compounded by the fact that he

had a great deal of trouble saying no. Despite the mounting pressures, he diligently tried to meet everyone's expectations. "I just don't want to let anyone down," he explained. "I don't want to disappoint anybody."

Now Keith Richardson—faithful husband, devoted father, conscientious servant of God—was burning out.

As the term implies, burnout is like a consuming fire. Fire can come externally—like a grass fire that roars down a hillside and engulfs a house, totally destroying it and everything inside. Or fire can start internally—such as with a faulty wiring system inside the walls—and end with the same disastrous results. It's the same with burnout. It can come from without or it can come from within. For pastors, it's usually a combination of the two.

Yet if we can get to the stress points soon enough, we can avoid the total burnout Keith Richardson experienced. The secret is to identify the problem, then to take action and make the necessary adjustments and changes, both externally and internally, before the fire gets out of control.

External Stresses

As a minister of the gospel, you surely face external stresses. They are unavoidable. You live in a society and work at a job that demands a great deal from you. The following are some of the external factors that are common among pastors.

1. *There is too much work to do*. Many ministers feel overwhelmed with all the work to be done and are continually frustrated because they cannot do it all. Because Christ touched every walk of life, many people feel that today's churches should be able to do the same. Indeed, most churches try. At the

same time, many people firmly believe it is up to
the pastor and his staff to get all that work done.
"We hired them," the people say. "It's their job."
But there is just too much to do!

2. *Confrontation is so difficult.* The inability to confront is a major factor contributing to stress and
burnout. Keith Richardson is a perfect example. He
had known for a month that he had to let his secretary go, he dreaded it terribly, and the matter continued to drag on unresolved. This pressure to
confront led to other internal stress factors such as
resentment (the senior pastor had dumped the un-
pleasant task in his lap) and unresolved anger (he
wanted the secretary to stay, yet he was being
forced to fire her).

3. *There is pressure to entertain the congregation.* The
entertainment syndrome has gotten really big in
some churches. In the competition to attract more
local Christians, there have to be more activities,
more music extravaganzas, and more pressure for
the pastor to be entertaining and "fun." The pressure is especially overwhelming on pastors who
serve alone. And to whom can the stressed pastor
turn for support? Certainly not to Pastor Jones
down the street. He is the competition.

4. *"Church shoppers" come and go.* A new "consumer
mentality" is becoming more and more prevalent
among church members. It used to be that people
joined a church and stayed there until they moved
away or they died. Now people shop around for the
religious services that appeal to them the most.
Rather than staying at a church and working to-

gether to resolve problems and difficult issues, they simply pack up and move on.

5. *Insecurity is a real pressure producer.* In many churches, as soon as problems arise, or if the church stops growing or is losing members, there is a move to get rid of the pastor. It's like firing the coach because he doesn't have a winning season. And even when the pastor's job isn't in danger, many churches are plagued from within with power struggles: How will the church's money be spent? What programs will be offered? What subjects will be addressed in the sermons? Insecurity breeds stress.

6. *Unresolved interpersonal conflict leads to stress.* Whether it is with a board member, a church member, a spouse, or whoever, the research indicates that pastors who have not been able to resolve their interpersonal conflicts suffer a tremendous emotional drain.

You might be saying, "Oh, yes, I have plenty of external stresses, more than you have listed here. The problem is, I can't do anything about them." When the pressures and stresses are part of your job, it certainly is easy to feel helpless against them.

So What Can You Do?

The fact is, some of the external stresses you face cannot be changed. The realities of the pastorate are there. When Keith Richardson looked at some of his external pressures, he decided it was hopeless, that there was absolutely nothing he could do. However, there really were some actions he could have taken. For example, he could have passed the direction of the youth choirs and the ensembles on to lay-people just as he had passed the children's choir on to his secretary. The reason he didn't was because he was afraid other people couldn't do quite as good a job as he could. He may have been right, but so what?

Keith could have also brought his financial problems to the board. As a matter of fact, he finally agreed to do this, but not until after his breakdown. With honesty and sincerity he explained, "I want to be effective here, but I need to face the fact that I may have to move away unless we can work something out. My family has been living in an apartment for five years now, and it's time we had a chance to buy a house." The board's reaction was, "Why didn't you say so before?" They not only responded by upping his salary, but one board member gathered together a group of families who offered to loan him enough money to make a down payment on a modest house. With his raise, he was able to make monthly payments to the lending families.

Finally, Keith could have talked to the senior pastor about his concerns over having to fire the secretary. When his feelings about this were finally brought out, the senior pastor was very understanding. The secretary was still let go, but Keith didn't have to be the one to give her the bad news.

All in all, the church was very supportive of Keith. They pulled together and realistically addressed the external pressures that were weighing so heavily on him.

With a bit of ingenuity and thought, you, too, will likely find you can do more than you realize.

Let's look at the first common factor we mentioned: *There is too much work to do.* What if the churches in your area determined to share the work load by complementing each other's ministries rather than competing? Let's say your church has a children's ministry that is operating on overload because you have so many young couples. You are struggling to build up an equally superior program for seniors. While continuing to accommodate the seniors you have, you could agree that this is an area of ministry for a sister church who already has a strong senior program. The fact of the matter is, very few churches can be equally strong in all areas, however hard they try and however hard their ministers work.

If you can overcome competition with the other pastors in your neighborhood, you might be surprised at how open and helpful and understanding other ministers can be. How about the laypeople in your church? Are you making full use of their gifts? You may be surprised at how open your church members are about shouldering their share of the work. And truthfully, it isn't scriptural for a pastor to take on all the responsibility. Doing so prevents other Christians from being challenged and growing. You, as minister, have an obligation to let your church know you are all in the ministry together.

You can help lessen the stress of expectations by learning to say in effect, "Hey, that's your expectation, but it's not mine. Your idea is a good one, but it's not for me to take it up and run with it. Let's talk to the board about involving some more of our laypeople in this project." You do not need to meet everyone's expectations, nor do you have to become personally involved in every worthwhile project that comes along.

External factors are a given. What complicates them is the less visible factors we carry around inside us, the internal stress factors.

Internal Stresses

A man we will call Bruce Martinelli was an exciting pastor. Bursting with almost frenetic energy, he was a fast talker and a quick thinker who had a million projects going all the time. He was the type of guy who literally bubbled over with infectious enthusiasm. When a large church in a major city decided to start a satellite church in another area of the city, they recruited Bruce as the new pastor. In the beginning his congregation was comprised of a dozen couples from the home church. But very quickly the fledgling congregation exploded. Four years later they had more than a thousand members who met in three buildings on twenty acres of land, and the entire project was paid in full. That was Bruce Martinelli, a true and tireless visionary who loved growth and movement.

Everyone loved Pastor Martinelli, and they never grew tired of listening to his spirited sermons. Although he enjoyed being around people, it was hard for anyone to tell what he was really feeling. He talked a lot, but he never shared much about himself.

Then one Sunday morning, Pastor Martinelli stunned his congregation by announcing from the pulpit that he would be leaving the church. Within a month he said good-bye to the congregation and went into business.

Bruce Martinelli had not succumbed to external stresses. It was the internal factors that proved too much for him.

Two years before, Bruce had come to Dr. Allen Doran uneasy and dissatisfied. "Our building is paid off," Bruce said. "My ministry is going well. What is there for me now? The challenge is gone."

And though few people knew it, Bruce had been nursing a deep hurt. He and his best friend, an influential architect and board member of his church, had had a painful disagreement. During an evening service open forum, the architect's teenage daughter stood up and insinuated that Bruce played favorites among the church members. The congregation was taken aback by the brash adolescent remark, but Pastor Martinelli, caught by surprise, was deeply troubled. Although he gave the girl as straightforward and honest an answer as he could, she and her father made no secret of the fact that they took it as a put-down. So devastated was Bruce that when he met with Dr. Doran the following week, that incident was all he could talk about. From that day on, Bruce constantly questioned his own judgment.

Bruce also worried that he wasn't a good enough counselor. He wanted to see immediate changes in people, and when it didn't happen that way, he grew impatient with them.

And although by almost any measure Bruce Martinelli was a successful minister, he never thought he was quite good enough. When a friend suggested he write out some of his very creative sermons, he replied jokingly, "I had my secretary type one of them up, but when I looked at it, it looked so horrible I decided I'd better never think of writing a book." With so much going for him, he still felt inferior and critical of himself.

Bruce wanted to do everything. Although the church was large, with more than fifteen hundred members, they had a church staff of only three. It's not that the church was unwilling to add staff members, it was that Pastor Martinelli didn't want anyone else. Delegating responsibility was a problem for him because he liked to make the decisions himself. And when his decisions were questioned, it caused him a great deal of inner turmoil that left him questioning his own abilities. Internal factors such as those that attacked Bruce Martinelli are insidious. They are harder to spot than external factors, harder to admit, and harder to deal with. When we look at our external pressures, we can say, "It's not my fault," but when we look at those pressures and stresses that come from within us, we feel guilty. We are convinced they are our fault, so we should be able to do something about them.

Internal stresses can be likened to straws on a camel's back. Because of our upbringing, our past experiences, certain character traits, perhaps even family dysfunctions, we have trouble handling the conflicts and events that come into our lives. Each one of those conflicts is like another straw piled on. The following are some of the common internal issues that really tend to add to the load.

1. *A high need for approval.* This makes it dangerous for us to risk displeasing anyone. When people come with their expectations, it is very hard to say, "No, I can't do that," or "I can only spend this much time on the project and no more."

2. *Workaholism.* A workaholic is forever driven to do more. A lot of time the church isn't asking their pastor to work all those hours and do so much. It's his feeling that he has to push, and the push comes from within himself.

3. *The "Messiah Complex."* This refers to the pastor who feels that unless he does a task himself it won't be done right. In essence he is saying, "I am the savior." It makes the pastor feel good and valuable to be so needed, and it certainly raises his self-esteem. But it is also an incredible pressure to have to live with.

4. *False guilt.* This is the affliction of the perfectionist pastor. We talked to one such minister who set himself an unrealistically high goal for winning people to Christ. He went into it full steam, knocking on every single door in his small town. A few people made professions of faith, but not one ever came to his church. Frustrated that he didn't see the demonstration of the power of Christ at work in him as he thought he should, he began to doubt that he was even saved. Consumed by false guilt, the man finally left the ministry.

5. *Discouragement.* This is a major complaint of pastors who come to us for counseling. Pastors are discouraged by the conflict in their churches, their wives are depressed because pastor husbands never seem to have enough time for them, pastors are so busy nourishing others they never seem to get any nourishment for themselves. And too many think of themselves as failures.

The first and perhaps the most important step in learning to handle internal stress is to learn to know yourself. Get acquainted with both your strengths and your weaknesses. Where do your vulnerabilities lie? What tendencies have you brought along from your childhood? Are there elements in your background that make you likely to be sensitive to a specific type of problem? What about your need for affirmation—do you feel you are getting enough? Do you have a high need for approval? Do you feel you have to always be in control? Do you struggle with confrontations?

Such a personal inventory requires a careful assessment of who you are, what your traits and tendencies are, and how it all interplays with your job as a pastor.

The Destructive Power of Expectations

Let's pause here to look at that super you from whom you have begun to expect so much. Check the statements below[1] that you feel describe the expectations you hold for yourself.

_____ 1. I should excel at everything.

_____ 2. I should not be tired.

_____ 3. I should not show my anger.

_____ 4. I should always be available to my church.

_____ 5. I should always be positive.

_____ 6. I should always be enthusiastic.

_____ 7. I should be a model of success for my congregation.

_____ 8. I should provide a good standard of living for my family.

_____ 9. I should be more productive.

_____ 10. I should exercise daily.

_____ 11. I should read my Bible and pray daily.

_____ 12. I should be creative in my sermons.

_____ 13. I should be friendly.

_____ 14. I should maintain a nice home.

_____ 15. I should be outgoing.

_____ 16. I should be businesslike, yet approachable.

_____ 17. I should not let problems get me down.

_____ 18. I should be more organized.

_____ 19. I should be able to handle all problems on my own.

_____ 20. I should prove myself in all situations.

_____ 21. I should have a vision for the church.

_____ 22. I should not be overweight.

_____ 23. I should not make mistakes.

_____ 24. I should never give up.

_____ 25. I should constantly push myself to my limit.

_____ 26. I should always finish what I'm doing before I move on to the next project.

_____ 27. I should develop new interests.

_____ 28. I should not expect rewards for my ministry.

_____ 29. I should be more hospitable.

_____ 30. I should attend all my children's activities.

_____ 31. I should be a friend as well as a parent to my children.

_____ 32. I should spend more time with my spouse and/or children.

_____ 33. I shouldn't have to ask for more pay. My value should be obvious to the church.

_____ 34. I should always look attractive.

_____ 35. I should reach all my goals.

_____ 36. I should never say no.

_____ 37. I should always feel sexually attracted to my spouse.

_____ 38. I should always feel accepted.

_____ 39. I should always feel competent.

_____ 40. I should use every moment productively.

If you have checked twenty or more sentences, your expectations are too high. You are setting yourself up for disillusionment.

Making Changes

So now that you have all this information, what does it mean to you? How can you go about making changes?

Begin by listing the external and internal factors that cause the stresses in your life. Start with the external, then move on to the internal. It might be easier to identify a trait by coming up on it from behind: What is its effect on you?

For instance, if you consistently end up taking on things for which you shouldn't be responsible, you probably have an overly strong need for approval. Or if you put off taking care of anything that smacks of confrontation, handling conflict and confronting others are factors that should be on your list.

Once you have identified the stress factors, you are ready to take action.

Handling the Stress Factors

To illustrate what it means to take action, let's look at how Keith Richardson worked through his inner conflict of avoiding confrontation. We started by pointing out to Keith that he had some options.

First, he could yield. Keith was a good example of one who yields in a conflict. He liked the secretary he was told to let go. He got along well with her and she was a great help to him. Although he didn't want to fire her, he yielded to the instruction to do so. In yielding, he was essentially saying to the senior pastor, "Okay, I give up. I'll do it your way."

The problem with yielding is that it keeps a person from being able to be himself. The one who yields feels restricted, resentful, and more pressured than ever.

Sometimes a person yields to another out of a high sense of respect for their relationship. Instead of risking getting into a big argument, the attitude is, "I'd rather just give in and let you have your way."

To yield is to seek peace at any cost—and the cost is often dishonesty and the hiding away of one's true self.

Another option Keith had was to determine to win. Keith could have gone into the conflict vowing, "I'm going to win at any cost. I'm going to overrule the senior minister and show him he's wrong about this secretary." The win option determines "I will have it my way."

For any of us, this is the least appropriate response. We can't really work toward a resolve unless we are communicating our openness to see the other person's side of the issue.

Keith could also have withdrawn. The problem with withdrawing is that it leaves the conflict unfinished and the anxiety building. The one who withdraws feels he isn't valuable, that he doesn't really count. He feels cheated, and that makes him increasingly angry.

A person can't get his own important, God-given needs met when he is always the one yielding or withdrawing from a confrontation. Such a person ends up very low on the achieved needs scale, and this leads to frustration. The feeling is: "If I never get my needs met, why do I want to be in a relationship with you?"

Since Keith's conflict was with the senior pastor, he had to retain some working relationship with him. Keith's approach was, "I'll do my job, but the less we see of each other, the better."

A fourth option for Keith would be to compromise. Compromise is taking the middle course. It's something like a horse trade with the two parties bargaining back and forth: "If you'll do this, I'll do that." Compromise is a move in the right direction, but it's not quite there. While it is a legitimate attempt to work out the situation, this approach is still based on conditions and trade-offs.

Finally, Keith could resolve. This option says, "Not your way, not my way, but *our* way. After all, we are a team here." Resolve requires real communication because it is based on both parties being able to see through each other's eyes. It is this option that is most likely to lead to a satisfying end to the conflict.

Every pastor comes into the ministry with one of these five conflict-resolution styles already established. Dave Congo tells of growing up in a home with two healthy brothers and a sister who was physically handicapped and bedridden. "My brothers and I would get into fights and arguments and have a great time duking it out. But my sister was very sensitive emotionally. If she heard us sounding angry and going after each other, she'd start to cry. Mom would say, 'Come on, you guys, cool it. When you can't get along you make it worse for your sister.' So part of what I learned when I was growing up was, 'Come on, Dave, be big enough to yield. Don't make trouble.' I learned to keep peace at any cost."

To this day, Dave struggles to feel free to be himself, to overcome his tendency to hide away part of who he is. "I don't speak up," he says. "I hold back even when I'm strongly feeling something that really needs to be shared."

Keith Richardson's approach was to yield in almost any situation where there was a difference or disagreement or conflict in his life. To help him deal with his self-doubt, his feelings of frustration, and his building anger, we talked about the importance of his working toward the resolve. We used the following analogy.

Suppose Keith and his senior pastor are out backpacking in the mountains, each in a different area. Keith takes out a sandwich and settles down to enjoy the peaceful scenery that stretches out so beautifully before him. Suddenly, he spots the back of a little cabin in a remote area in a valley below. When he looks more closely, he notices that the place is in real need of work. There's a broken-down corral fence by the back door, and firewood and trash are strewn around the backyard. In fact, the place seems a real mess.

Meanwhile the senior pastor is on the other side of the valley looking down at the same cabin through his binoculars. He, however, is getting a front view. From a cute little duck pond flanked by a beautiful woods of birch trees, a shady path winds up to the front door. At the windows lace curtains softly rustle in the breeze. "What a beautiful hideaway!" he whispers in awe. "I'd love to go down there sometime and just relax."

As evening approaches, both men come down into a little town at the foot of the mountains and meet for dinner.

"Where were you backpacking?" the waitress asks them.

"Up the mountain about fifteen miles from here," the senior pastor tells her.

"That's a very remote region," says the waitress. "The only people living up there are an old couple. Years ago they built a little cabin in a valley completely surrounded by the mountains."

Both pastors respond that they saw the cabin.

"It sure was a beautiful setting," Keith says. "It's too bad the place is so run-down. That broken-down fence, the junk scattered around . . ."

"What are you talking about!" the senior pastor exclaims. "That cabin is wonderful, and so well-kept. The duck pond, the path from the birch woods, the lace curtains in the windows. . . ."

At this point we asked Keith, "Which of you was right about the cabin, and which was wrong?" The answer, of course, is that both were right. Keith's perspective and feelings, though different from those of the senior pastor, were every bit as valid.

Resolve

Don't be shocked or surprised when a conflict or disagreement arises between you and someone else on your staff. It's inevitable. You are going to see some things from different perspectives; you're going to have different points of view. So begin by erasing the unrealistic expectation that conflict isn't going to happen to you. Only when you do that are you ready to move ahead.

Start by stating your perspective of the situation. It might help to practice before you actually confront the other person. With Keith, we role-played how he could ask his senior pastor to come around to his side of the mountain, to stand alongside him and see the conflict from his perspective. "Before anyone talks to the secretary, I need to share with you where I'm coming from," he said in his practice session. "I want you to know how difficult this is for me. I have lost so many nights of sleep over this matter. Just the thought of having to deal with her ties me in knots." Then Keith went ahead and stated the reasons why he didn't agree with the decision to let the woman go: "Look at some of the problems I'm facing," he said. "Not only am I going to lose my secretary, I'm going to lose my choir director. This is going to add still more stress and work to my already overstressed and overworked life."

After you've stated your position to the other person, let him or her ask you questions.

Then it is your turn to go around to the other person's side of the mountain. You might say, "Maybe I don't understand where *you* are coming from. I respect you and care about you, and I want to hear this from your point of view." For Keith Richardson, this approach was a great relief. Understanding it was the first step in changing his lifetime style of avoiding conflict.

The Last Straw

Certainly no one factor, either external or internal, is by itself a crushingly big deal. The problem comes when all the stresses and pressures pile up together and weigh us down for a period of time. If I carry fifty straws for one intensive week, then I unload them and kick back and relax, it's not that bad. But if I have been carrying those fifty straws all year without any relief, the next one becomes like the proverbial straw that broke the camel's back.

Be Creative

It's time for you to find some creative, workable answers to your own pressures. You have already taken the first step of identifying the external and internal factors that lead to stress in your life. The next step is to talk about those stress factors. If you speak it out loud to someone you trust, that person may be able to help you put the situation into perspective. No one is able to be objective with his own issues.

The third step is to gain as much insight as possible: Why is this an issue? ("I didn't get enough approval when I was a child, so now I have an especially high need for it.") Where is it coming from? ("My father was the one in control in my family when I was growing up. Perhaps that's why I now feel I have to control everything.") Are you struggling with a messiah complex? ("How can I turn it over to anyone else? I can do it best.") The more you know about yourself, the easier it will be for you to make appropriate change.

The fourth step is to begin to change your thinking. You can do this through Scripture, and you can do it through the feedback of others who are more objective than you.

The fifth step is to take action. Some external factors really are unfair—too low a salary, no day off, the demand that you constantly be on call—and those factors won't go away just by wishing they would. Usually, God doesn't remove the stress factor by prayer alone. He expects you to do something about it. Aristotle once said: "We are what we repeatedly do." You can use this principle to your advantage. What you begin as deliberate behavior changes eventually become who you are.

Now look back over the list you made of your own pressure factors and ask yourself:

- Which of these factors must I accept and cope with as best I can? Put an A beside each of these factors.

- Which can I work toward changing? Put a C beside each of these.

Now look back at the first item you marked with a C. Ask yourself:

- How might I go about making some changes here? What specific action might I take?

- To whom do I need to talk about this?

- To whom do I need to say no?

- Whose help might I enlist to help relieve some of this load?

As you think of answers to these questions and possible solutions, jot them down. Don't limit your ideas; try to think creatively. Write down the good, the bad, and the crazy! Using the model we set forth for handling the stress of conflict and confrontation, you can walk through each of the stress factors you have on your list.

Too many of us live with all kinds of unnecessary pressure. We convince ourselves that somehow we are doomed to be in that stressful situation. But once you determine to make changes, you will likely be surprised at the power your determination will give you. To make up your mind to accomplish a specific action and to know you have Christ with you puts you in an extremely powerful position.

Don't settle for a passive approach to your external stress factors. Do all you can to be sure you are seeing the matter from a Christlike standpoint, then take action and do something about it.

When the stresses begin to weigh you down, plan opportunities to get away. Put a priority on achieving a relaxing change of pace. We see a good example of this principle in 1 Kings 18. On Mount Carmel, the prophets of the idol Baal had prayed and pleaded from morning until night for Baal to hear them and prove his power by sending fire to consume their sacrifices. Although they jumped on the altar and slashed themselves with knives and cried out to their god, nothing happened. Then it was Elijah's turn, and God certainly didn't disappoint him. When the fire fell from heaven, it not only consumed the sacrifice but the water that filled the trench around it—and even the very stones of the altar. What a triumphant victory!

But when Queen Jezebel heard about what had happened, she was boiling mad. She sent a messenger to convey her vow to Elijah that he would be dead by the next day. Now Elijah had just seen God prove His power in a staggeringly dramatic way. Yet rather than claiming this power for himself, Elijah panicked. He ran off into the scorching desert and hid. "Lord," he cried, "take my life!" The pressure on him was so great that he preferred to die alone in the desert rather than face it.

It was at that lowest point that an angel of the Lord came to Elijah. The angel didn't chide him, nor did he try to counsel. No "Boy, are you ever messed up spiritually" came from the angel. What he did say was, "Here's some food for you to eat, Elijah. Now lie down and rest."

When any of us gets really stressed, perhaps even close to

burnout, we need support. But we also need time to get away and regain our equilibrium.

You can go a long way toward releasing your internal pressures by eliminating the "shoulds" in your life. Reexamine the expectations you have heaped on yourself.

The reality of being in the ministry is that there are peak times that are going to be very stressful for you. Certainly it's important to accept this fact and decide how you are going to adjust to it. But it is also vital that you set aside time for balancing out those stressful times with opportunities to relax.

Stress Isn't Always Bad

You may be a person who basically feels your capabilities are high. Sure, you know you have some weaknesses, but overall you are a strong person. If you are in a job where the demands are even higher than your capabilities, you will likely feel stretched and challenged. That's okay. It's good to be pushed and stretched a little beyond ourselves. It's healthy to learn to say no when you need to, and when and how to draw others in when you need help.

Nor is stress only produced by negative factors. Any overload of change, even good change, produces stress.

Rat Race or Relay Race?

In some ways a rat race is similar to a relay race. Both involve a lot of activity and both use up a great deal of energy. In both it is obvious that things are happening. But there is also a significant difference: In a rat race, people are running here and there and everywhere, while in a relay race people are running in an organized way on a prescribed course. When dealing with stress, it is important that you be running a relay race. To avoid being trapped in a rat race, ask yourself: Do I know who I am? Do I know my strong points? Am I moving in line with my strengths? How do my strengths fit in with the goals I've set for myself? To make yours a relay race, you need a clear direction with a goal at the end.

As in a relay race, you have the advantage of the freeing reality that you aren't supposed to run all the laps yourself. Give it your all when you run your lap, but when yours is over, be ready to pass the baton on to the next runner. If you are to be able to cope effectively with the stresses in your life, the ability to give it your all then to pass the baton on is critical. There may be another person to whom you can pass the baton, or it may be that you will pass it over to the Lord: "You know about this family I've been working with. I did everything I could for them, but now I've got to go home and be with my own family. I can't help them any more right now, so I'm releasing them into Your hands."

You need not let your stress factors get the best of you. Take action and take charge.

4

Mastering Your Mammon

I n Matthew 6:24 Jesus said, "No man can serve two masters; for either he will hate the one and love the other, or else he will be loyal to the one and despise the other. You cannot serve God and mammon." The Lord desires and demands our undivided devotion and commitment to Him. We cannot be preoccupied with mammon (which can be translated as money, possessions, or other material things). If we try to do it any other way, it will eventually lead to frustration.

Let's face the facts. Pastors can be really poor money managers, just as they can do a fantastic job in this area. If you are like the majority, you fall somewhere in between the two extremes. The following financial checkup will help you determine how you measure up as a manager of your money.

Financial Checkup

If married, husband and wife should take the checkup independently and compare answers and scores. Answer each question as it is written. If it says, do you have "written goals," that is exactly what it means. Please be truthful in every answer.

---

*Financial Checkup was taken from the *Personal Finance Course*, by Ethan Pope (Hattiesburg, MS: Financial Foundations for Living), 45–46.

Points

_____ You are able to pay your credit card bills in full each month.
[4 points for every month you have paid them in full during the last 3 months.]

_____ You operate your family finances on a workable written budget.
[10 points for a yes.]

_____ You consistently save money in a savings account, money market, or investment vehicle.
(We are not talking about savings being allocated for a pension/retirement plan.)
[4 points for every month you have saved during the last 3 months.]

_____ Your family has written financial goals on paper in the following areas:
☐ Debt
☐ Giving
☐ Saving
☐ Vacations
☐ Car Purchase
☐ Retirement
[1 point for each area in which you do have written goals.]

_____ During the last 12 months, you have not decreased insurance coverage (life, property, health, or disability) due to financial limitations in your budget.
[5 points for a yes.]

_____ You have the equivalent of _____ months salary in savings and available to pay for any repairs, medical expenses, or family needs.
[10 points for anything more than one month.]

_____ You have no past due bills (not credit card) presently outstanding and you have not received either a past due notice or a telephone call from a collection agency within the past six months.
[10 points for a yes.]

_____ You do not have feelings of depression due to your money situation.
[5 points for a yes.]

_____ You have not cut back on your giving during the last 12 months.
[10 points for a yes.]

_____ You have a current will that includes all the following information:

- Your present address.
- Name of primary and backup guardian for your children.
- Name of your executor and a backup executor.
  [5 points for a yes.]

_____ You or your spouse have all your important papers (insurance policies, investment information, debt information, wills, birth certificates, etc.) located in one (or two) place(s) and *you* know exactly where to find them.
[5 points for a yes.]

_____ You or your spouse have filled out a personal balance sheet within the last 12 months and your spouse has seen it.
[5 points for a yes.]

_____ You have feelings of jealousy or greed toward family members, friends, or associates. You covet what other people have.
[5 points for a no.]

Your points _____

Mark your score below:

0	10	20	30	40	50	60	70	80	90	100
——— Critical Condition ———					Danger	Poor	Fair	Good	Excellent

How was your score? Any room for improvement? If you are like most of us, you could work on some areas. Certainly no one is perfect in dealing with his family finances, but none of the questions on this checkup is unrealistic. Every one represents a very important aspect of good financial management.

A Pastor's Responsibility

You as a pastor have your own unique financial stresses with which you must deal every day. You are called upon to socialize with every level of society, from the person who is consistently out of work to the corporation president. Because you are watched by all, you have to be careful as to the kind of car you drive, the house you live in, the clothes you wear. If your car is too nice, some will think the church is paying you too much. If you drive an old, beat-up car, some will think you are a poor testimony in the community. There will never be a time when everyone is completely satisfied with the image you are presenting.

But your financial responsibility goes beyond your own personal finances (not all of it fairly placed on you, by the way). If the financial base of a church is expanding, the members pat each other on the back. But if it is going through a financial crisis, they consider it the pastor's fault.

In many church building programs, for example, it is the pastor who becomes the chief financial adviser and full-time general contractor for the construction. And what about sermons on tithing and giving to support God's work? The complaint is always that the pastor either preaches too much about money or that he doesn't talk about it enough. Yet when couples come to the pastor with their financial problems, he is expected to have all the answers.

The Positive Side

Despite all this, you have a wonderful opportunity to model good financial management and financial integrity to your congregation; you have a chance to be salt and light in a world that is desperately crying out for responsible guidance. What an opportunity you have for ministry when you can stand in the pulpit and offer biblical principles for money management and illustrate them by saying, "This is what my family does, and it works." What an op-

portunity for discipleship when you can feel the confidence
to disciple key men in this very important area.

Financial Planning Concepts

If you are experiencing financial stress and frustration,
don't despair. By applying the following eight action
points, you will be better off spiritually and financially
than 95 percent of all Americans today.

Action Point #1: Acknowledge That God Owns It All

In Psalm 24:1 we read: "The earth is the LORD's, and all
its fullness, / The world and those who dwell therein."

That's right. Everything belongs to God. It is 100 percent His. Not even a part of it is yours or mine. It all belongs
to Him alone. But you do have a responsibility, for you are
God's steward over the possessions He has entrusted to you.
And one day you will be called upon to give an accounting
of how you have managed God's possessions: "For we must
all appear before the judgment seat of Christ, that each one
may receive the things done in the body, according to what
he has done, whether good or bad" (2 Cor. 5:10).

The teaching that God owns it all is the ultimate foundation in Christian stewardship and financial management
from a biblical perspective. So it is here that we must begin, with the correct attitude toward our possessions.

Action Point #2: Establish Family Goals

Every one of us, whether single or married, needs clear
direction in life. Goals will help give us that direction.
Proverbs 21:5 says: "The plans of the diligent lead surely to

plenty, / But those of everyone who is hasty, surely to poverty."

Do you have goals for your life? Surveys reveal that more than 90 percent of us do not have written life goals. It's really quite amazing, don't you think? Before an airplane pilot starts the plane engine, the course has been carefully plotted. The same is true of a ship's captain. If you expect to get anywhere in life, you, too, need to lay out a clear course of where you are going.

If you are married, here is an interesting exercise for you and your spouse: Write down your top three financial goals for your life. Without showing your list to your spouse, ask her to do the same. If you have clear family goals, the two lists should be the same. If you have never discussed family goals with your spouse, you may be very surprised at how different your list will be from hers. For example, your two lists might look something like this:

	Husband	*Wife*
Goal #1	Buy a new car	Get new carpets for the house
Goal #2	Take a ski vacation	Get new clothes
Goal #3	Pay off mortgage	Save for kids' college expenses

It's not that either of you is right or wrong in your goals, it's just that there hasn't been clear communication between you about your respective needs and where you are headed as a family. Goal setting is simply a communication project.

Also, if you establish your goals, you are more likely to accomplish them. I have found that when my wife and I did not have clear goals, we were more likely to be frustrated over money issues in our family. Now that we have established our goals, we are both headed in the same direction.

Action Point #3: Control Your Debt

If there is any one area that can lead to financial bondage, it is the abuse of credit cards. In my opinion, every credit card should have the following warning printed across it in red ink: WARNING! THIS CREDIT CARD CAN BE HAZARDOUS TO YOUR FINANCIAL FUTURE!

Unfortunately, pastors aren't exempt from credit card abuse. In fact, some people will tell you that pastors have some of the worst credit ratings in the country.

Credit cards, if properly used, cause no problem. It is when they are overused and abused that trouble starts. The first sign of credit card trouble is when you receive a credit card bill you cannot pay in full. That's right. You should be able to pay off every one of your credit card bills each month. If you can't do it, stop and ask yourself: "Why can't I pay off this bill?" The answer will be: "Because I have lived beyond my God-given means." If you are earning $25,000 in annual income, but you live as if you are earning $30,000 and are financing the extra $5,000 with credit cards, you are indeed living beyond your means. If this is true of you, it's vital that you exercise discipline in your spending. Even better, perform major surgery on your credit cards and cut them in half—then throw them away.

From a financial perspective, financing purchases on credit cards is a foolish mistake. If you keep an average ongoing balance of $1,000 every month on your credit cards and continue to pay the minimum payment each month, you are making an incredible financial mistake. If you doubt this, consider what one credit card is costing you during your working life: A $1,000 balance at 18-percent interest costs you $180 each year in interest alone ($1,000 x 18% = $180). If you paid off your credit cards and paid yourself that $180 every year, just look what you would accumulate during your working life: At $180 a year for 40 years with an interest rate of 7 percent, you would end up with a grand total of $35,934.32!

Now, I'm not saying you shouldn't use credit cards for the sake of convenience. If you pay your credit card bills in full each month, in most cases there is no interest charged. Your goal should be to use your credit cards, but never allow them to abuse you.

What about Borrowing to Buy a Car?

Buying a car on credit is as American as apple pie. But is it the wisest way? Let's look at the figures: If you get a $10,000 car loan at 10-percent interest, your payments will be $253.63 for 48 months, or four years ($253.63 x 48 = $12,174.24). Here's how your expenditure breaks down:

$12,174.24	Total Cost of Car
− $10,000.00	Principal
$ 2,174.24	Interest You Paid on the Car

"But," you may be saying, "I have no choice. How else could I buy a car?"

Well, let's consider another possibility. Let's assume you can continue to drive your old car for three more years. Suppose you begin to pay yourself a car payment into your savings account. If you saved $253.48 and your savings earned 6 percent each month, in 36 months you would have accumulated approximately $10,000. Compare this to using debt to buy your car:

Cost using debt	$12,174.24	($253.63 x 48 months)
−Cost using cash	$ 9,130.68	($253.63 x 36 months)
Savings to you	$ 3,043.56	

That's right! By paying with cash, $3,043.56 less will be coming out of your checking account to pay for the very same $10,000 car! And here is an extra motivator for you: If you saved more than $3,000 every time you bought a car, every fourth car you purchased would be paid for by the savings from the first three cars. This is what being on the earning side of interest does for you as opposed to being on the paying side.

How about a Home Mortgage?

Good question. Did you know that a $75,000 home mortgage at 10-percent interest for 30 years will end up costing you $236,944.80 during the lifetime of the loan? Staggering, isn't it? Here's how I came up with that figure: The monthly payment for P & I (Principal and Interest) is $658.18 ($658.18 x 12 x 30 years = $236,944.80). You can determine how much your own home will cost you by following the same formula. Simply take your monthly payment for P & I and multiply it times 12 and then times the number of years you will have your loan:

$_____ x 12 (months) x _____ Years $_____
    Monthly Payment   Years of Loan   Your Total Cost
       for P & I

A fifteen-year mortgage will end up costing only $145,071 ($805.95 x 12 x 15 = $145,071). By having a fifteen-year mortgage instead of a thirty-year mortgage, you would save a whopping $91,873.80!

There are ways to prepay on your mortgage and save literally thousands of dollars. You would be amazed at how much savings you can realize by adding an additional $25 or $50 each month to your payment. An excellent book called *The Banker's Secret* can be a helpful tool in learning more about this area. For example, for a 30-year, $75,000 mortgage at 10% interest, *The Banker's Secret* says, "If you make small investments (pre-payments) in your mortgage—as little as $25 each month—you'll save more than $34,000 in interest on that $75,000 example and you'll reduce the loan's term by over 5 years. Just $100 a month, and you'll end up $78,000 richer—12.5 years sooner!"[1]

As an ordained minister, you have a special advantage in the area of interest deductions. In a procedure commonly called "double dipping," you receive housing allowance income "tax-free," and you are allowed to deduct any mortgage interest you have paid during the year. This gives ministers a tremendous tax advantage. Understand, though, that interest written off on your taxes is not a dollar-for-dollar write-off. Nor does it always mean that it is to your advantage to keep your mortgage. (Check with your financial adviser, CPA, or the IRS concerning the specific details of this aspect of tax preparation.) For most people, the best plan is to get out of debt as fast as possible.

Church Debt

This chapter would not be complete without discussing church debt. Let's assume your church is considering a new building program. It has been proposed that the church borrow $1,000,000 from a local bank. The new loan can be obtained at a 10-percent interest rate for a 30-year mortgage. To see the impact of the loan, let's first determine how much your church will be committing to pay each month for the mortgage payment. A $1,000,000 loan at 10-percent interest would require a monthly payment of $8,775.72. (Just think what the monthly commitment would be for a 5-, 10-, or 15-million-dollar building program!)

What will the total cost of the building program be? Here are the figures: $8,775.72 (monthly payments) x 12 (months in a year) x 30 (years) = $3,159,259 (total payment).

$$\begin{array}{rl} \$3,159,259 & \text{Total Cost} \\ - \ \underline{\$1,000,000} & \underline{\text{Original Loan Amount}} \\ \$2,159,259 & \text{Interest} \end{array}$$

That's right! Your church will pay over $2,100,000 in interest! My personal opinion is that such a mortgage is not a wise use of God's resources.

Let's look at another option. How long would it take your church to save $1,000,000 if you began putting aside the equivalent of the previous mortgage payment of $8,775.72 and earned just 7 percent on your investment each month? You would have your $1,000,000 in eighty-eight months (7.33 years).

Now, here is the exciting part of using the savings approach. At the end of 7.33 years, you not only have the money for your building, you also have $8,775.72 you can set aside every month for the next twenty-three years. Instead of paying this money to a bank for that period of time, you can use the money for ministry. If you can't wait seven years to save for a building program, pray and ask God to accelerate the giving so you can obtain the cash more quickly.

Nowhere in Scripture do we see God's people using debt to finance God's objectives. Instead, we find God's people (and sometimes nonbelievers as well) providing the material resources to accomplish God's objectives. (Consider Nehemiah rebuilding the wall, David and Solomon constructing the temple, Noah building the ark, and the mass exodus from Egypt.)

Not only has debt abuse destroyed many marriages and businesses, but churches, too, have succumbed to out-of-control debt. Proverbs 22:7 says: "The rich rules over the poor, / And the borrower is servant to the lender." Wise Christians will recognize God's Word as their ultimate guiding light and plumb line in this as in all other areas of life.

Action Point #4: Be Sure You Have Adequate Insurance Coverage

Most families need four different types of insurance protection: health, property, disability, and life. Let's consider these one at a time.

Health Insurance

You are at great risk if you don't have proper health insurance. With the rising cost of health insurance, one way to decrease your expenses is to raise your deductible from $100 or $250 per family member to, say, $1,000 per person. What this allows you to do is to decrease your monthly or quarterly premiums. You will be responsible to cover 100 percent of the initial $1,000 in medical expenses, but at the same time you will have medical coverage for a catastrophic problem. (*Note:* If you have a choice, let your church give you health insurance as a benefit. If you have to pay for it out of your salary, you also have to pay taxes on the salary you used to buy it. However, if the church provides health for you, they must provide it for all their other employees as well.)

Property Insurance

You need to have coverage on all your personal property, such as your home and car. If you rent or live in a parsonage, you still need to buy renters' insurance for your contents. The parsonage building is usually covered under the church's policy, but it is unlikely your personal belongings are covered unless you have your own policy.

In some states, ordained ministers receive a discount on their car insurance. When you are checking, be sure to tell your insurance agent you are a minister. The company will possibly rate both your cars with a "pleasure" rating rather than a "business class" rating. This will definitely save you money, in some states anywhere from 5 percent to 20 percent.

Disability Insurance

Do you have coverage in the event you become disabled? You should. Even if you are disabled, your bills will still come due. Yet, in insurance, this is the area most often neglected. You are especially at risk if you opted out of the Social Security program.

Life Insurance

How much life insurance coverage do you need? The general rule of thumb is this: Take your annual income and multiply it times seven or ten. Here's an example: A pastor who earns $20,000 would need at least $140,000 ($20,000 x 7) and at the most $200,000 ($20,000 x 10).

Let's assume you have $200,000 in insurance coverage when you die. Your spouse would receive $200,000 in insurance benefits from your policy. If she were to carefully invest the insurance money, your family could receive annual interest payments of anywhere from $14,000 (7 percent return) to $20,000 (10 percent return). Keep in mind that this is just interest. She wouldn't even be touching the principal. Of course, as needs arise and inflation goes up, the principal could always be tapped. However, in the short term, the needs of your family would be provided for.

The number-one objective in buying insurance is to obtain adequate coverage for your family. The type of insurance (term versus whole life or universal life) is not the most important aspect. For most families to obtain adequate coverage, they will have to buy all (or at least some) term insurance. (Term insurance is "pure" insurance. Whole life is insurance combined with a savings vehicle.)

Many sincere Christians have asked, "But isn't insurance gambling? Wouldn't I be wagering my $500 against their $90,000 that my house might burn down this year?" The answer is a resounding "No!" Insurance is *not* gambling. Gambling creates a risk; insurance simply covers a risk. When a person bets on a sporting event, there is no risk until the bet is placed. If you don't gamble, you have no risk. However, there is the risk that your house might burn down or that you might die unexpectedly whether you have insurance or not. Insurance simply covers an existing risk, unlike gambling, which creates its own risk. No, insurance is definitely *not* gambling.

Action Point #5: Operate Your Household on a Budget

I define a budget as taking your projected income and deciding ahead of time how this money will be given, saved, and spent. (Note the priority.)

For years I have taught a budget system called a MAP—Money Allocation Plan. Unfortunately, space does not allow me to explain this simple system. However, I believe that to be successful, the key ingredients of any workable budget system must include the following five basic ingredients:

1. *You and your spouse must plan the allocation together.* Budgeting is not the job of just the husband or just the wife. Pray about it together and work on it together.

2. *Plan your allocations for the month and year at home.* Don't wait until you are in a clothing store and spot a big sale to decide how much you will spend for clothes.

3. *Update the allocation plan once a week.* Don't wait a month or a year. If you are updating your MAP once a month, all you are doing is tracking your past expenses. A MAP is primarily intended to look ahead, not behind. It should influence your money management today, tomorrow, and next week.

4. *Don't worry about tracking every dime or dollar you spend.* A good system always looks at the big

picture. Maybe you will allocate $50 or $100 every month into each spouse's personal allowance category. This will be "spending money" not accounted for in any way. This takes away the detailed record keeping that can drive some people nuts.

5. *Evaluate every expense at least once a year.* Write your life goals out, and then make sure you are using your budget to accomplish those goals. For example, one life goal may be to help your children pay for college expenses. But if this isn't written into the monthly budget, it's nothing but a dream.

A budget becomes meaningful when you see it as a tool to help you accomplish what you really want in life. For every category and every expense, ask the question, "How does this fit into our overall family goals?" Cable television is a good example. Sure, you may be able to afford the $20 every month, but could the annual savings of $240 be better used for a family vacation or educational videos or a family project?

Budgeting also takes the guilt out of spending. When the money has been allocated for clothing, entertainment, furniture, or vacations, go out and spend it and enjoy! After all, that's why it's there.

A wise minister will determine to be a careful money manager. A budget system should allow you to be more generous in your giving, consistent in your savings, and, in your spending, will give you true freedom.

Action Point #6: Consider Your Ways

Do you earn money and put it into a pocket or purse that seems to have holes in it? Do you always seem to be living in need or want? If you are, the Bible says to consider your ways. The prophet Haggai, talking to the nation of Israel (and to us), said,

> Now therefore, thus says the LORD of hosts:
> "Consider your ways!
> You have sown much, and bring in little;
> You eat, but do not have enough;
> You drink, but you are not filled with drink;
> You clothe yourselves, but no one is warm;
> And he who earns wages,
> Earns wages to put into a bag with holes."
> Thus says the LORD of hosts: "Consider your ways!"
> (Hag. 1:5–7)

You see, the nation of Israel had been disobedient to the Lord. They were not being faithful in their giving, and they were reaping the consequences of that disobedience. Malachi tells us they had been presenting animals for sacrifice that were sick, lame, and blind (Mal. 1:8)—a practice that was anything but honoring to the Lord. Malachi warned that if they tried to pay their taxes with the sick, lame, and blind, their governor would not accept it. He would kick them out of his presence by the seat of their pants!

How do we dare offer God our leftovers? He deserves the firstfruits from us, the very best we have. Does your checkbook reflect this priority in your life? Are you faithful and generous in your giving? If anyone should be a faithful and generous giver, it's the pastor.

Action Point #7: Begin a Consistent Savings/Investment Program

Start saving regularly. Your first savings goal should be to accumulate one to three months' salary in an emergency fund. This money can be used for unexpected bills or family needs. If you encounter an unexpected bill and you have no emergency fund, what is your option? Right! Credit card debt.

After you have established an emergency fund, you are ready to enter an investment mode. One key principle of investing is to diversify. What this means is that you don't want to have all your invested money in one investment. You might have your investment divided up into several areas, such as a money market fund, a CD, a mutual fund, and U.S. Savings Bonds. I especially like a concept I call "steady plodding." Let me explain. Did you know that if you saved/invested two thousand dollars every year for forty-five years, you could potentially have savings of more than one million dollars? It's true. Here's how it works:

Amount Invested Every Year for 45 Years	% Interest Earned	Total in Fund after 45 Years
$2,000	5%	$ 319,400.31
$2,000	7%	$ 571,498.62
$2,000	9%	$1,051,717.47
$2,000	12%	$2,716,460.07

Now, I'm not saying you should accumulate a great deal of money. I'm just showing that it doesn't take large savings every year to accumulate a relatively good-sized investment account that will allow you to meet your God-given goals and objectives in life.

Action Point #8: Buy and Learn to Use a Financial Calculator

You might think this is an unusual action point, but I believe it to be one of the most important of all. Learning to use a financial calculator will allow you to oversee numerous financial decisions in your life and in the life of your church. If you will set aside three to five hours to learn how to use one, it will have a tremendous effect on your financial life. All you have to do is read the manual carefully and work out each example or problem. Then do some practicing on your own.

When you are faced with a financial decision in the future, you will be better prepared to do the right thing. For example, if you will be needing $28,000 in ten years to send your child to college, you will be able to calculate just how much you need to save each year (or each month) in order to accomplish your goal. A financial calculator is without a doubt a worthwhile investment.

The challenge I want to leave with you is to assess your money-management style, see where you need improvement, and then take action. It will take time and effort, but it could just change your life and ministry.

---

*This chapter was contributed by Ethan Pope, CFP and founder and president of Financial Foundations for Living. Most of the concepts in this chapter were taken from *Personal Finance Course*, by Ethan Pope. For additional information about this course you may write to: Ethan Pope, Financial Foundations for Living, P.O. Box 15356, Hattiesburg, MS 39404.

5

Pastor, Counselor

Everyone from employers to neighbors to advice columnist Ann Landers tells hurting people, "You need counseling. Go see your clergyman. He'll help you." In fact, according to a study conducted by the Gallup Organization for the National Association of Chain Drug Stores, 70 percent of the people questioned rated ministers as important sources of information and advice. Of the women questioned, 77 percent nominated pastors.

Whether you want to counsel or not, whether you think you're good at it or not, one thing is sure: people are going to come to you for help and advice. Some will only need a listening ear, a pat on the back, and a few words of encouragement and assurance. Others will require immediate, intensive therapy.

What's a minister to do? If you are a strong, confident counselor, you may not need help—except perhaps for suggestions as to where to find a few more hours in your day.

"In my opinion, some pastors need to back off a little bit on the amount of time they spend counseling a person," advises Dick Meier. "It just isn't realistic for him to try to do it all. He could meet a person for an initial session and provide short-term counseling as well as some follow-ups;

but if a person can't be helped in six sessions, consider the possibility that he or she needs to be referred to a professional."

Even pastors who have strong counseling skills—or perhaps *especially* them—will struggle with the questions of where to find time to counsel everyone who comes to them for help and at what point to draw the counseling line. So how much time *should* a pastor spend? "Not more than half a day a week—one day maximum," advises Dr. Frank Minirth. And if that half or whole day doesn't allow enough time to counsel everyone? "Refer," he says.

"A pastor who schedules four to eight hours a week to do counseling will often end up putting in twelve or more hours," Dr. Paul Meier adds. "This is because pastors are usually the first person church members go to when they have an emergency. That's why we recommend four to eight hours of regularly scheduled counseling appointments with an hour a day left unscheduled to handle emergencies or to catch up on telephone calls."

"Certainly a pastor needs to be flexible," Dick adds. "Sometimes you may know you are this person's only chance for help, that he or she just won't go to see anyone else. In that case, you'll do whatever you have to do."

What about Referrals?

So you need to be ready to counsel, you need to be prepared to refer, and you need to be flexible. Sounds good, but it can be a pretty confusing order. Under what circumstances should you refer a person to someone else? To which specific professional should you refer a particular client? How do you go about referring a person? All good questions. Let's consider them one at a time.

When Should You Refer?

Basically, you are responsible for referring a person whenever it is in his or her best interest that you do so—when, for whatever reason, you are unable to best serve the needs of that person. Doing this is simply obeying the golden rule.

Of course, whether or not a referral is in the best interest of a specific counselee is often a matter of opinion. There are certain situations, however, in which you should definitely refer a person:

- when that person is suicidal or homicidal.

- when you are too limited in time to adequately deal with him or her.

- when the situation is beyond your ability to handle it.

- when the problem involves anything medical.

- when the person who has come for counseling has an extreme problem (such as someone who is psychotic, neurotic, or alcoholic).

- when violence is involved (such as child abuse or wife battering).

The following profiles can help you identify those with conditions that require the help of a professional counselor:

1. People who are suicidal often exhibit

   - feelings of hopelessness and helplessness.

   - a lack of desire to live.

- an inability to control the urge to hurt themselves.

- previous attempts to end their lives.

- specific, thought-out suicide plans.

2. Homicidal individuals often demonstrate

- strong feelings of anger they don't feel able to control.

- definite plans to injure or kill another person.

3. In psychotic men and women, you will often see

- an inability to think, respond emotionally, remember, communicate, interpret reality and/or behave appropriately.

- evidence of delusions or hallucinations.

- behavior that is grossly disorganized.

4. Neurotic people often show

- such symptoms as extreme anxiety, hysteria, obsessive-complusive behavior, and phobias.

- depression so extreme that it renders them unable to function in normal daily activities.

5. People who need to be checked by a medical doctor may

- complain of extreme or frequent headaches, migraines, or other physical discomfort.

- have serious physical problems that affect their ability to function normally.

- experience an abrupt weight gain or loss.

- complain of poor physical health or such symptoms as a loss of appetite or an inability to sleep.

6. Substance abuse may be evident in people who

- misuse and abuse alcohol.

- misuse and abuse prescription medications.

- misuse and abuse illegal drugs.

7. Realize that you are being presented with problems that are beyond your ability to help when

- you meet with individuals or situations that are too intense (for whatever reason) for you to adequately be of help.

- you are too tired emotionally, physically, or spiritually to remain objective and helpful.

- a person continues to struggle with an emotional problem from the past and doesn't seem to be improving with your help.

- a person is having a difficult time coping at work, socially, or at home, with even basic responsibilities.

Certainly, you should be aware of those situations you are required by law to report to the proper authorities, such as incidences of elder abuse, child molestation, or child abuse. (Requirements can vary from state to state. Be sure you are clear on those that pertain to yours.) Before people open up to you about such a situation, let them know you cannot withhold that information. Tell them it's not up to you, that by law you will have to report it. But please understand that this requirement is in the best interest of both your clients and those who are affected by their actions. Let your counselees know it is for their own good, then assure them that they can have the loving power of God and God's forgiveness supporting them all the way.

Even when you decide to continue to counsel a person yourself, professionals can be invaluable to you for medical questions, evaluations, psychological testing, and assessment, as well as for legal and ethical advice. Not only may such professional advice help enhance your client's treatment, but it can also provide you with legal and ethical safeguards. So consulting with others can benefit both you and your counseling client. The services we provide at various Minirth-Meier clinics, for example, are unique because they are based not only on sound medical and psychiatric principles, but also on a solid foundation of Christian principles and beliefs.

To Whom Should You Refer Your Client?

Once you know *when* to call, the next question is, *whom* do you call? And a good question it is, too, for a number of options are open to you. Here are some of the professionals you might consider and a brief description of each:

Psychiatrist

A psychiatrist is a licensed physician who specializes in the diagnosis, treatment, and prevention of mental and emotional disorders. A psychiatrist's training includes four years of college, four years of medical school, a year of internship, and three years of psychiatric training.

A Christian psychiatrist is first of all a Christian; second, a medical doctor specializing in the physical disorders that affect mental processes; and third, a counselor. Some

Christian psychiatrists also have some theological seminary training.

It is important to remember that the psychological, physical, and spiritual parts of a person all affect one another. Because there are medical origins or repercussions to many disorders that on the surface appear to have only a psychological—or even a sinful—base, a medical doctor who specializes in psychiatry can be very helpful. If your client has a mental or emotional disorder and there is a possibility that he or she may require hospitalization or prescribed medication, this is the specialist to consult.

Psychologist

This professional is a person who holds a doctoral degree in psychology and has two years of supervised work experience in the treatment of mental disorders. Because psychologists are not medical doctors, they cannot prescribe medication. Yet they have almost as much training as psychiatrists. Besides having approximately ten years of education, a Christian psychologist may also have some theological or biblical training. Psychologists are excellent counselors and are better at psychological testing—such as conducting vocational, personality, and premarital evaluations—than are psychiatrists.

Counselor/Therapist

A person who is a certified counselor or therapist is trained to assist clients in the treatment of mental disorders. "Psychotherapist" is a general term that does not specify the level of educational training, which could range from a B.A. or B.S. degree all the way up to a doctorate. A Christian therapist could have a Bible or theology degree, a secular degree, or both. Whatever the degree, he or she will base counsel on Christian principles. That is why referrals should only be made to Christian therapists rather than to those who have a non-biblical agenda.

A therapist is often as effective a counselor as a professional who carries the title of doctor in medicine or psychology. However, therapists may have to refer their clients to others for testing and will certainly have to do so for any treatment of medical situations.

Medical Doctor

This is a person who has earned a medical degree and is trained to handle general or specialized medical problems.

A Christian medical doctor is a wonderful person for you to have on your list of referrals. He or she will know what to look for medically and—because physicians are more trained in the system than are most pastors—can assist you in properly referring difficult or puzzling cases.

There are also counselors who are competent professionals who just happen to be Christians. They don't integrate their Christianity into their practices, but at least they are in the same camp as you. Although they may not say much about it, they are able to relate to their clients from a Christian standpoint. These could be used as a last resort, but a Christian therapist whose worldview and agendas for therapy are all integrated through a biblical grid is certainly preferable if one is available in your area.

We should also mention a category of people who can sometimes act as most satisfactory assistants: laypeople from within your own church body—a deacon or elder, a friend of the troubled person, or perhaps just a concerned fellow Christian. As a matter of fact, it would seem that the people God uses most often to help others are ordinary

Christians. For this reason, pastors have a responsibility to train their congregations to appropriately meet the needs of others. That's not to say nonprofessionals should attempt to do the work of professional counselors. They shouldn't. But for encouragement and support, and day-by-day loving and the modeling of healthy relationships, lay Christians can be extremely effective. Just be certain that you not encourage laymen and women, however sincere and well-intentioned, to drift into areas they are not really prepared to handle.

Before you add a specific professional to your list of referrals, be sure you know enough about him or her to be able to refer with confidence. You might want to compare notes with other pastors. Certainly, take into consideration any comments former clients of that person might share with you. By all means make an appointment with the professional you are considering, or at least talk to him or her by telephone. Some of the things to find out are whether or not the professional:

- knows Christ as Savior.

- is gentle and kind.

- believes the Bible from cover to cover.

- integrates Scripture into his or her counseling.

- believes that salvation is by grace through faith as explained in Ephesians 2:8–9.

- looks at divorce from a biblical viewpoint if marriage problems could be an issue.

- looks at the role of self-concept biblically—that is, that the concept of self is based not on what we do, but on our position with Christ.

- has balance in his or her own life and doesn't deal in extremes.

- lives what he or she counsels—that the counselor's own life shows a mentally and spiritually balanced person.

How Do You Go about Making the Referral?

Once you have decided that a specific client should be referred and you have selected the professional to whom you will refer that person, your next consideration will be how you go about making the referral.

If you have gotten to know several local physicians, psychiatrists, psychologists, and counselors, and if you have built some rapport and established a working relationship with them, you will find it much easier to make referrals. It will also help if you have learned the particular ways each of these professionals prefers to have clients referred to him or her. If you haven't asked, by all means do so.

Talking directly to each of the professionals on your list of referrals has another advantage: You can determine to what degree each one is open to keeping you involved in the treatment process. It helps when you work with those who are willing to work with you.

When you are ready to make the referral, telephone the professional and give the client's name and any other pertinent information you may have. Follow up your call with a letter of referral, and be sure to keep a copy for your own files.

It is important that you make it a practice to keep notes of counseling sessions for each client you see. Include such information as the dates you see the person, the topics you discuss, your recommendations, and any referrals you make. On page 90 is a sample sheet you might want to use for your counseling notes.

If you determine ahead of time the circumstances under which you will refer, the professionals to whom you can refer, and the referral process you will use, you will be ready to match a client up with the professional who can help her the most.

Counseling Women

Day after day, clergymen sit in uninterrupted privacy with women who trust, admire, and rely upon them. It is a powerful position to be in, one that creates a constant pull toward even greater intimacy with women who crave compassion, understanding, attention, and affection.

As a pastor, counseling is an important part of your job. When your client is a woman, counseling must be approached with caution and wisdom. We human beings are more creatures of emotion than of logic. The reports of pastors who let their involvement with their clients go beyond that of counselor, becoming involved with the women who come to them for help, are both distressing and alarming. Almost across the board these are men who meant well, men who really wanted to help. And they are intelligent men who knew better. In many ways they are no different from you and me.

Women who come to you for guidance and advice are often extremely vulnerable. It is your responsibility to make certain that your sessions with them remain on a professional level.

Problems can start long before there is any sexual involvement. In an article in *Psychology Today*, Peter Rutter, M.D., states: "Every woman I've spoken to who engaged in forbidden-zone sex described the immeasurable *nonsexual* value she felt the relationship had attained before any sex-

Counseling Notes

Name of client: _____

Major topic(s) discussed:

_____
_____
_____

A. Current situational issues:

_____
_____
_____

B. Past issues:

_____
_____
_____

Client suicidal? Yes _____ No _____
Scheduled return date: _____
Advice given:

_____
_____
_____

Cautions given:

_____
_____
_____

Signature: _____ Date: _____

ual behavior took place. All felt they acceded to sex as a way of maintaining a relationship that had extraordinary importance in their lives."[1]

There is a fine line between being a trusted confidant and becoming emotionally involved. Sometimes a step over that line is barely discernible, something as innocent as a special hug or a gentle caress or holding hands during prayer in a private counseling session.

If You're Already There

For a pastor who has already become sexually attracted to one of his clients, Dr. Frank Minirth has the following five suggestions:

1. *Begin with the spiritual.* Scripture has great restorative power. Memorize such verses as these: "I have made a covenant with my eyes; / Why then should I look upon a young woman?" (Job 31:1); "No temptation has overtaken you except such as is common to man; but God is faithful, who will not allow you to be tempted beyond what you are able, but with the temptation will also make the way of escape, that you may be able to bear it" (1 Cor. 10:13); and "Abstain from fleshly lusts which war against the soul" (1 Peter 2:11b).

   "It's true, you know," says Dr. Minirth. "Lust allowed to exist and grow really *is* going to wage war! It helps me to remind myself of the tremendous mission at stake, a mission far greater than whatever my own needs are at the moment."

2. *Move to the concrete.* Such practical steps as putting a window in the door of your counseling room

can prevent the problem from surfacing in the first place. Dick Meier says he always left the door between his and his secretary's offices ajar. "Never see a woman for counseling when the secretary is not present," cautions Dr. Paul Meier. "And never counsel a woman alone in her home."

3. *When a problem does come up, deal with it directly.* For instance, if a woman counselee tells you she is drawn to you personally you might respond with, "I think the feelings you say you have for me are coming from deeper within you. It's not actually me at all. Let's look at where these feelings are really coming from." Usually the woman has a driving need to be intimate emotionally, often because of having been ignored and/or abused by her father. She is grasping for a way to get her powerful needs met, and society has taught her that the way to do it is physically. Her emotions buy into it and so do her hormones—a volatile combination for sure.

4. *Be accountable to someone.* Have someone to whom you are accountable, and get together with that person each week. You are much less likely to act on your impulses if you are talking about the situation with someone else. One warning here: Don't share your feelings of attraction with your client. It isn't fair to tell her, "Hey, I'm attracted to you." It puts too much pressure on her to deal with your problem.

5. *You may need to get counseling yourself.* It may be that you would do well to look into talking to a professional counselor. You may have some areas of

needs and codependency you should be working through.

Some pastors ought not counsel at all. They can be more helpful by offering well-informed referrals. An objective counselor can help you determine whether or not you are one of these.

People will look to you, their pastor, for help, guidance, and advice. They will need to draw upon your God-given wisdom and insight. A challenge to be sure, but one you can meet. By planning ahead, you will be able to determine the best way to meet the needs of hurting people around you.

BLEST BE
THE TIES

6

The Marriage Relationship

F or twenty-four years Jeanine served alongside her pastor husband, through thick and thin, in good times and bad, through great expectations and utter discouragement. Then one clear autumn morning, when times were neither particularly good nor particularly bad, she crawled into bed and swallowed a handful of sleeping pills. Jeanine never woke up. "Why?" her distraught husband asked as he shook his head in confusion. "What could have possibly made her unhappy enough to do this?"

Like many devout, hard-working ministers, Jeanine's husband had no idea of the stress his wife had endured.

While such an extreme response is rare, pastors need to take into consideration the facts of life under which their wives live.

Expectations from Everyone

So what is a pastor's wife to be? Easy. The blueprint is on page 98.

Look anything like your wife? If so, she is in a class by herself. For most pastors' wives, the myriad of expectations thrust upon them are impossible to attain.

Author Mary Bouma, herself a pastor's wife, recalls that not too many years ago ministry couples were hired as "two

BLUEPRINT FOR THE IDEAL PREACHER'S WIFE

Escape Valve—To relieve tension without blowing her top.

Radar Mind—To know exactly where her husband is and what he is doing.

Mouth—Always smiling, always encouraging, speaking only cheerful words, never gossiping.

Computer Brain—Able to produce clever lessons for every occasion, talks and devotionals on any subject, cute ideas for parties and socials, inspired methods for encouraging and cheering her husband.

Eyes—One eye in front for watching the music as she plays the piano, one in the back to keep an eye on her perfect kids in the front pew.

Ears—Equipped with automatic strainer to strain out any information that shouldn't be repeated.

File Cabinet Mind with
1–Everything her husband might forget,
2–Recipe file with dishes that cost next to nothing but taste great,
3–Never-fail information on child rearing,
4–Miscellaneous file on everything anyone will ever want to know.

Hair—Left side in fashion, right side conservative. Naturally beautiful all over.

Arms—One to keep her house neat at all times, one to keep her family clean and well-dressed, one to work at the church, one to raise perfect children.

Clothes—Not too new, not too old. Not too bright, not too dull. Not too fancy, not too plain. But always, always neat.

Body—Tireless, strong, resistant to every ailment.

Figure—Not too heavy, not too thin. Not too glamorous, not too matronly.

Feet—to work . . . and work . . . and work . . .

for the price of one."[1] While times and expectations have changed, many congregations still have an agenda for the minister's wife—even many that insist they don't. Bouma tells of a young woman who commented wistfully, "We have been married just three months. While my husband was on staff, we dated, became engaged, and finally married. The congregation has set us up as models of romance, dating, and ideal newlyweds. It's difficult to maintain the image of perfect love when you're human and facing normal problems."

It is indeed.

And why should pastors' wives be forced into such a mold? Why should they be looked upon differently than other women in the congregation? If they want to do extra in the church, fine. But the Lord has not given any of us the spiritual gifts to do everything. If spouses are required to do what they are not really capable of doing, they end up stressed and, in time, burned out.

Like you, your wife goes through the painful process of discovering that not everyone is going to like and accept her. If she is going to be happy in her role as minister's wife, there has to come a point where she can remove herself from the expectations thrust upon her and determine for herself: "Just who am I? How has God gifted me? How do I want to function in my personal life? How do I want to function in the church?" Only when she has found her answers will she be able to move beyond the expectations of everyone around her.

Disappointment in Herself

Many pastors' wives start out full of idealistic pictures of what their church relationships will be like. But soon they discover they need to set limits.

"I wasn't prepared for the power people," says Claudia Root, whose husband pastors a large church in Southern California. "At our first church there were people who lavished me with gifts, but the day came when I found out all those gifts had strings attached."

Loneliness

It has been said that pastors' wives are the loneliest women around. And there is much advice given on how to deal with this loneliness: Should she have friends in the church? (If she does, people might say she is cliquish.) Is it okay to have one special friend? (Others might resent her exclusiveness.) Should she find her friends outside the church? ("She doesn't think we're good enough for her!" some church members are sure to say.) How should she pick her friends? (As if there is only one right way.)

Claudia Root told of one woman who was especially friendly to her at a time when she really needed a friend. "It turned out all she wanted was to get information out of me she could gossip about."

Although it hurts to discover that someone you consider a friend is taking advantage of you, it helps to look at an experience like Claudia's as an opportunity for growth. "It made me more wary, more careful in selecting friends," Claudia says. "But it didn't make me unwilling to take a risk." She went through a period where she thought, "Well, I guess a pastor's wife just can't have friends." But after a few months she decided, "I'm not going to be like that. I'll just be more careful whom I choose."

Your wife should have friends. She needs them. If she has friends within the church, people will have a chance to see that she has good relationships with other people. Will there be criticism? Probably. But so what? It isn't fair to allow hurtful words to make her lonely and unhappy. She, like you, needs to learn to forgive and move on.

Some wives are afraid that if they let people get too close, their weaknesses will be found out. People will discover they aren't perfect. "That's all true, but I've learned to reach out anyway," says Claudia Root. "I'm a normal person with good points and bad points. I want people to see that."

Loneliness also comes as a result of a pastor's irregular hours. "I was going through a period when Jerry was gone a lot," Claudia recalls. "I had just had my first baby and I was starting to resent being home alone. When I complained about it to another pastor's wife she told me, 'I used to be like that. What helped was to realize my husband would *rather* be home with me. He was doing all he could to be home. Now, instead of complaining and grumbling, "Why's that guy so late?" I turn it around and pray, "Lord I don't know why he's not home yet, but I do know he'd like to be here. Something must have come up, so I'm praying that you'll be with him and give him wisdom."' That really helped me."

The Times, They Are Changing

The role of the pastor's wife has changed a lot in the past generation. Many women today say they feel the freedom to be whatever and wherever God leads them. Some are fully involved in the church, some involved very little. A few are not involved at all.

Mary Sue, the wife of a pastor in Oregon and a very independent person in her own right, teaches history full-time at a state university. "Sure, people sometimes complain," she says. "They say the place for a pastor's wife is by his side. I tell them, 'My husband is the pastor. I'm a teacher. I have my own career.'"

Indeed, a major reason why some of the long-held expectations are being lifted off pastors' wives is that so many are working outside their homes. Author Bonnie Rice reports that 21 percent are employed full-time. And while slightly more than half (51 percent) of the pastors' wives surveyed consider themselves full-time homemakers, more than a third (39 percent) of these are employed part-time.[2] These busy women don't have time to play the piano for Mrs. Johnson's Sunday morning class or to head up the women's work at church.

Besides providing extra income for their families, an outside job allows a pastor's wife to have a life of her own. The negative side is that it can drive her world still further away from her husband's. It also raises the level of criticism from within the church ("She's more concerned with material things than with the ministry."). It's up to your wife to decide what is right for her, and it's up to you to support her decision. Whatever role your wife plays in your ministry, she does carry a special responsibility. "We wives are in a position of leadership," Claudia Root points out. "We have to be careful to not always speak out, nor to say exactly what we think all the time. I have learned through painful experience to 'Wait patiently on the Lord.' The times I have not done that, when I have failed to use discretion, have been the times I've learned the biggest and hardest lessons about being a pastor's wife. I feel a constant pressure to carefully weigh what I say because I realize I have a position that is different from that of other women."

Listen to Your Wife

In most cases, a pastor's wife is far more aware of her husband's susceptibility to stress and burnout than he is. In Genesis 2:18, God said: "It is not good that man should be alone; I will make him a helper comparable to him." Your helper—that's what God intends your wife to be. Yet too many pastors won't let their wives *be* helpers.

Do you have trouble accepting help from your wife? If so, you need to foster your own marriage to the point where there can be an ongoing evaluation between the two of you. Learn to listen to her input and to process it. Tell yourself, "I'm going to look at this objectively," and then do it.

One more suggestion: Put a high priority on helping your wife be healthy and happy with herself. Wives who feel good about themselves give their husbands the best support—regardless of how involved they are in his ministry.

Between Husband and Wife

In many ministers' families conflicts are routinely swept under the rug. Instead of working together toward resolving their problems, too many get hung up trying to paint issues as black or white: One person is so dogmatic about how a thing is to be done that there can be no compromising about it. The other feels unable to fight it, and either goes off angry or becomes passive-aggressive.

A common complaint voiced by the wives of ministers is, "I don't feel valued as a person." Lynne Hybels is a good example. In *Sunday to Sunday* she writes that at one point in their marriage, her husband told her, "People are dying and going to hell, and you want me to stay home and hold your hand?"

How could Lynne answer a question like that? "If I said yes, I'd sound blatantly selfish and unspiritual," she said. "If I said no, I'd be a liar. Therein rested my dilemma. I knew my minister husband was uniquely gifted to reach the spiritually needy people of our community, and I wanted him to do that. I also wanted a healthy marriage. Unfortunately the two goals seemed mutually exclusive. . . . There I stood—one timid woman against the ministry, the church, the myriad of needy people, perhaps even against God Himself."

Bill, Lynne's husband, was to later say, "One day I was reading Ephesians 5:25: 'Husbands, love your wives, just as Christ also loved the church and gave Himself for her.' I'd always thought the ultimate test of my love for Christ was my degree of devotion to the ministry. Suddenly, however, I understood that God's commendation was based on a much broader criterion. I was called to honor Him in all areas of my life. That meant I was every bit as accountable to God for the quality of my marriage as for the quality of my ministry. It seemed so obvious; I was embarrassed I hadn't come to this understanding sooner."[3]

Pastor, you are commanded to love your wife just as Christ loved the church. The message is clear: You are accountable to God for your marriage relationship. If it isn't what it should be, it's up to you to make changes.

For Lynne and Bill Hybels, finding answers wasn't easy. By the time Bill finally started giving more attention to their marriage, Lynne had detached herself from him emotionally. But Bill didn't give up. He began to court her again. Together they took steps toward healing. Lynne wrote: "Establishing priorities demands tough choices. It means bucking habits that are entrenched. The answer is to build a solid relationship based on open communication. Bill and I began with prayer. We learned effective communication techniques, and we committed ourselves to carefully planned and protected times together. It took perseverance, but we are thankful that God has helped us remake our ministry marriage."[4]

For some ministers, the conflict between husband and wife takes a different form: she resents that he is more visible than she is. If your wife is struggling with this, she needs a sense of recognition and prestige for herself. It is vital that she have an identity of her own. She needs to feel she is important for who she is, not just because she is the pastor's wife.

"A pastor's wife needs to be reminded that performing behind the scenes is no less a ministry than performing on a platform," Lorraine Meier says. "Even when her gifts aren't visible, they are still significant and valuable. The church needs her too. The body of Christ needs her."

Encourage your wife to reach out and find some area in which she can be involved and can contribute, where she can be herself.

Sometimes the value of a wife comes in the face of adversity. "After Dick's heart surgery, I detected a change in him," Lorraine Meier says. "He seemed more caring, more appreciative, more concerned about what I would do if he weren't here."

"Talking about the possibility of my dying was very tough," Dick added. "I badly needed Lorraine's emotional support. Just facing the possibility made us realize how important we were to each other. It gave us a glimpse of what a void there would be if we were without one another."

An older pastor from a different church in town took Dick to lunch one day. The minister's wife had recently died of cancer. For two years, he told Dick, she had suffered terribly. And through it all, he was constantly by her bedside. His ministry, which had been the main focus of his life, faded into the background. At the end of her life, he told Dick, his wife said to him, "These two years have been the best two years of our lives."

"How can this be?" the man asked her incredulously.

She took her husband's hand and said, "Because of our fellowship together—the loving, the caring, the talking. Yes, these two years have definitely been the best."

The pastor, his eyes filled with tears, looked straight at Dick and said, "Don't wait. Make *these* your best years."

Dick Meier walked away from that lunch shaken, but he took what he had heard seriously. Today he tells other ministers, "It's easy to say, 'One of these days we'll do things together, but right now we've got to climb the ladder of success.' Well, you just may find out that ladder is leaning against the wrong wall."

In his dissertation, Brian Newman speaks of his survey on marital satisfaction. Although admittedly limited, his survey reveals that those couples who reported spending the most leisure time together, away from the rest of the family, also reported stronger and happier marital relationships in other areas. Their shared leisure time together was an important pivotal point in how happily and successfully they communicated and resolved their conflicts.

Today, when so many pastors' wives are going out and doing their own thing, it's especially important that husband and wife come together and agree on some activities they can do as a couple. You say your interests just don't overlap? Then perhaps you need to agree to share in each other's interests. You might say, "This time we'll do what you like to do, next time we'll do what I like to do." And while you're participating in each other's activities you can continue to look for one you will both enjoy together. It's got to be a give-and-take process.

If there is a single secret to staying happy together, perhaps it is this: develop something special you can enjoy together in your leisure time.

The Positive Side of Being the Pastor's Wife

Claudia Root recalls that after her husband had been in the ministry about five years, they went to a dinner where they were seated next to an older pastor and his wife.

"What do you think about being a pastor's wife?" the older woman asked Claudia.

"Oh, I love it!" Claudia said.

"Just wait," the woman replied ominously. "Just you wait!"

Claudia recalls coming home and promising herself, "I am never going to be like that. I'm going to really work at making this the most wonderful life I could possibly lead." Ten years later, she feels she has kept that promise. To her, it is a choice. "There are things in my past where I could choose to go down the bitter path, or I could choose to learn from the experience and go down the positive road. It's my choice."

A pastor's wife can be a wonderful encourager. Because of her high visibility, encouragement from her can go miles. While she has to be cautious about some things, she can be perfectly free in her uplifting of others. What an opportunity for service!

There are other positives too. "How many other wives get a chance to be so involved in their husband's work?" Claudia asks. "I get to do a lot of things with my husband most wives can't do with theirs. Jerry and I are doing what we believe in, and I can be as much a part of it as I choose."

Most pastors' wives find a great deal of significance— even enjoyment—in their role. In a survey conducted by National Association of Evangelicals (NAE), half of the respondents said they love being married to a clergyman. Four out of five saw their role as God's will for their lives, and fully 60 percent felt fulfilled. Seventy-seven percent indicated that their congregations give them freedom to be themselves.

In summary, Kenneth Crow, professor of sociology at Mid-American Nazarene College in Olathe, Kansas, who helped analyze the study, said, "The overall pattern revealed in our study of pastors' wives was quite positive."

In fact, the study reports that the longer wives served, the more satisfied they were. Of the wives who had under five years in the ministry, 57 percent felt fulfilled. But as the time rose above twenty years, 94 percent felt fulfilled. Forty percent of the wives under the age of thirty felt they were competing with the congregations' demands on their husbands. By age forty, it had fallen to 18 percent. Eighty-five percent of the women who responded said their marriages were healthy and compatible. Four out of five had confidence in their husbands' fidelity, and nearly two-thirds said their children enjoyed being ministers' kids.[5]

That's a pretty positive picture!

What Can You Do for Your Wife?

Although the positive side is bright, your wife does need help and support from you. Close to half the pastors' wives surveyed said they experienced frequent emotional ups and downs. Even worse, one in six felt she was "close to burn-out." Younger wives, especially those with children at home, were much more likely to describe their role as "stressful," "hurtful," and "frustrating." Nearly half said they needed "a real vacation," and 56 percent said they could use some rest and relaxation. Half said they needed help coping with stress.[6]

The good news is that there is a lot you can do to help

reduce your wife's stress level. It all begins with setting the proper priorities in your own life.

Setting Priorities

Where is your wife on your list of priorities? Most pastors' wives claim their husbands place them no higher than second place—not behind God, but behind the ministry. Little wonder so many feel resentful. When that resentment grows into anger, they are riddled with guilt.

You say it's not your fault your ministry takes first place in your life? You say the church won't let you set your own priorities? Sounds like you need to learn to say no. Perhaps you could remind your board and your congregation that the church is a body. Some members are hands, some are legs, some are eyes, some are toes (1 Cor. 12:12–31). You can't be all parts of the body; you shouldn't even try. Agreeing to do everything cheats others of their opportunity to serve. And it keeps you from being able to set your priorities appropriately.

The following will all be true if you and your wife have realistic expecations.

She Won't Have to Feel Like a Martyr

It's all right for your wife to take breaks. It's okay for her to say no, even to good things. Although there was no end to the needs Jesus encountered during His ministry, He didn't meet them all. He didn't heal everyone. At one point Jesus got into a boat and told His disciples, "Let's get away from these people. I need a break." Encourage your wife to set her own priorities in a realistic way. And when she says no to some involvement, stand behind her and back her up.

She Won't Feel She's Your Unpaid Employee

Some pastors are so used to administrating and to telling their staff and secretary what to do that when they come home they go right on giving orders. When you come home, be sure to take off your pastor hat and put on your husband hat. Instead of demanding and warning of consequences, make suggestions and share your desires and wishes. Set up a pattern of teamwork with your wife. Talking and thinking in terms of rules and ultimatums and dogmatism only builds resentment. (The same is true within your church, by the way.)

She Will Be Able to Communicate with You

One of the things we hear so often from pastors' wives is the extreme loneliness they feel because their husbands are never around. Yet how can a wife complain, especially to anyone in the congregation? When she feels suffocated by the life she believes is dictated for her, she has no one to whom she can turn. Is there anything you can do? Yes. You can help your wife by allowing for good communication between the two of you.

Communication is something of a buzzword right now. You've heard about it, you've read about it, you've probably talked about it yourself, maybe even from the pulpit. But even when a pastor knows a lot about the principle, he may not be able to really communicate with his wife. When she starts talking to him about her feelings and concerns, he can feel so threatened he just shuts down.

We referred before to Dick and Lorraine Meier's method of communication, one that has become a cherished part of their lives—their talk dates, something Dick calls "empathetic communication."

"Every Tuesday, Thursday, and Saturday we walk together and talk," Dick explains. "It's probing communication where Lorraine and I check on each other's feelings and needs on a personal, intimate level."

The goal of good communication is for both you and your spouse to be able to share your feelings about an issue, and for both of you to give the courtesy of listening to the other without being defensive. To accomplish this, it is important that you be committed to acknowledging your wife's feelings.

"One of our big rules is *do not give advice unless it is requested*," Dick says. "If Lorraine says, 'I really feel sad. A woman who works with me was diagnosed with cancer,' I have to be careful not to jump in and tell her what to do. She doesn't want advice; she wants her feelings to be understood. This is so hard for the typical man to understand because men tend to be more solution-oriented than women.

"Once Lorraine shared with me that she felt like she was an invisible person. I was amazed. She explained that when she shared her feelings with me, I wouldn't acknowledge them. Instead I'd jump in with, 'Here's what you should do.' I was so busy being Mr. Advice that I ignored her emotional side." After Lorraine explained what he was doing wrong, Dick listened and started to actively work at understanding her.

"Try to crawl into your wife's skin and feel what she is feeling," Dick advises. "Pick up the look on her face, the sound of her voice. Look her in the eye and show through your body language that you are listening and understanding."

How well do you and your spouse communicate? To help you determine, answer the following five questions as honestly as you can:

_____ My spouse and I often linger after meals, enjoying the opportunity to share with each other.

_____ We have at least two times a week when we set aside time to talk about our concerns and desires.

_____ I am aware of my spouse's emotional needs.

_____ I feel my spouse is aware of my emotional needs.

_____ My spouse and I don't get confused about each other's daily schedules because we keep each other informed.

Were you able to say yes to all five statements? If so, you and your wife are likely communicating well. If not, look back at those statements you couldn't affirm and come up with ideas for specific things you can do to improve your communication.

Here's another suggestion: First, list three areas in which you feel you and your wife do communicate well. Next, list three areas in which you feel your communication is falling short. As you read over the two lists, appreciate the progress you have made and determine to work on the areas that are lacking.

She Will Feel Loved and Nurtured

The way to keep from running into emotional walls or falling into wrong relationships is to have a strong marriage. This is precisely why priorities are so vital. It takes time and effort to keep your marriage strong, but it is well worth the effort.

Nurture a vibrant love in your marriage. Marriage is like a garden. If you leave it alone, weeds will grow so thick they will choke out the flowers. A good marriage also takes work. Problems need to be weeded out while they are small and manageable. You cannot focus on church work and figure your marriage will take care of itself. Make time for love. Make time for humor. Make time for fun.

Dick Meier says, "Love is like a triangle made up of three distinct sides. One is agape love—commitment love, love that may even mean sacrifice. The second is phileo love—a high-grade friendship. The third is eros love—romantic love.

"Phileo love is what is usually missing in a marriage because it requires time. You have the church, community interests, and hobbies; your wife has the kids and the house, her activities and maybe her job. Your lives are worlds apart with little overlap. Once again, it's a question of priorities. Set aside time to play games together, to make popcorn and watch television together, to go to car shows or concerts together. Build fun time right into your schedule.

"Eros love is more sensual. It includes sexual love, but it's more than that. It is also hugging and kissing, touching, holding hands. Ask your wife what romance means to her. To the typical woman, it's not what happens in bed. It's what happens all day long—phone calls to each other, hugs, playful teasing, a gentle attitude. Brag on your wife (yes, even from the pulpit!). Get out of town with her. Enjoy her company, and let her enjoy yours."

Demonstrate your love by helping your wife be herself. Some wives feel as called to the ministry as their husbands do. They want to be involved. Others feel called to be just wife and mother. They don't want to be as involved at church. In which class does your wife see herself? Discuss it with her. You may be surprised at what she has to say.

One pastor came to see us after his wife of fifteen years suddenly packed her bags and left him. When the shocked man asked her what happened she told him, "For fifteen years I've been under a terrible strain. Never have my needs been met. Never have I been nourished emotionally. All this time I've been playing a role that doesn't fit me, and I just can't take it any more."

"Why didn't you ever tell me?" the pastor asked.

"Because you never asked," his wife told him. "You were never around long enough."

How emotionally aware are you of your wife and her needs? To help you determine, check off the statements below that are true of you.

_____ In the last week my wife and I had an in-depth talk that didn't include such issues as the job or the kids. We talked about ourselves and our feelings.

_____ My wife is aware of my most worrisome prayer burdens and I am aware of hers.

_____ My wife and I pray together at least four times a week (not counting before meals).

_____ I know my wife's greatest struggle(s).

_____ I am aware of my personal priorities as well as those of my spouse because we discuss them regularly and strive to help each other achieve them.

_____ My wife and I talk about our expectations for her participation in the ministry, and we agree on how much she will be involved and in what areas.

_____ We spend leisure time together at least twice a month.

_____ We have many happy memories of the leisure time we have spent together.

_____ I don't let anything interfere with my day off.

———— Both my wife and I feel comfortable talking about our sexual life.

———— Romance is definitely in our relationship.

———— We "date" on a regular basis.

———— We have a good balance between the time we spend talking about church business and the time we spend talking about personal matters.

———— I have a male support person or persons to whom I can talk openly about church problems so that I don't have to always dump problems on my wife.

Did you find some statements you couldn't check? Then you have pinpointed areas that need work.

She Will Not Feel Starved for Time with You

In their survey of ministers' wives, *Leadership* asked this question: "What would you want us to tell your husband if he would never know you said it?" Almost everyone answered, "Tell him I need more time from him than I get."[7]

Only twenty-four hours are in a day, and those hours only stretch so far. Don't allow your wife to be squeezed out by other things, no matter how worthwhile those other things may be.

She Will Help Break Down Walls That Have Built Up Between You

If barriers are already there, it is vital that the two of you talk together about your hurt and anger. You need to share your feelings without attacking each other ("I feel pressured," "I feel I'm being used"). It is important that you listen empathetically, that you climb into each other's skin.

If there is anger between you, you might try writing an "anger letter" to each other. Take your time. It might take you a week to complete, just adding a few lines each day. In your letter, unload your memories, perhaps going back many years. Write: "I felt discouraged when you . . . ," "I felt frustrated when you . . . ," "You really hurt me when . . ." Be specific. Then, at an agreed upon time— maybe over coffee and a slice of your favorite pie—share your letters. Read one all the way through without interruption. Then come back and look at the issues *that are still going on* ("You don't give me any time." "You never show any interest in what I'm doing."). One issue at a time, try to resolve them all: "What can we do about this? How might we change that?" As for *past* issues, remember that they cannot be changed. All you can do is discuss them, try to understand them, forgive them, and move on.

But the present can be changed, and that is where your efforts should be concentrated. Part of forgiveness is a hope for the future. If you love someone, you don't want to go on hurting her.

She Will Be Willing to Go with You for a Marriage Tune-up

Marriage tune-ups aren't intended for couples with terrible problems. They are for husbands and wives who just want to stay on track. Many churches offer marriage tune-up days or weekends. Not only will it be good for you and your wife to go for your own sake, but your attendance will provide wonderful modeling for other couples in your congregation. You can set an example, not of perfection, but of being willing to work to keep your marriage relationship strong.

Your wife needs you. She needs to know she is high on your list of priorities. She needs assurance that she can depend on your emotional support. And she needs your help in keeping her own stress level under control.

Offering Emotional Support

"For years and years we didn't have a ladies' missionary group in our church because I had seen so many of them end up being nothing but a gossip time," said Lorraine Meier. "Finally a group of ladies got together and presented an outline of what they wanted to accomplish. Dick said, 'Okay, but I want you to know I don't expect Lorraine to have to attend. If she chooses to come, fine, but she mustn't be required to.' I really appreciated that support from him."

Not only can you support your wife emotionally by acting as a protective buffer for her, you can also brag on her and express your love to her publicly. By letting your congregation know that the two of you have a close, loving relationship, you will be helping them as well.

When there are decisions to be made that will affect the family, let them be family decisions. One pastor walked into his house one evening and announced, "In two weeks we're moving to another state." He had been feeling out new churches in various areas of the country for over a year, yet his wife knew nothing about it. Can you imagine how this affects a family, especially when there are teenagers at home? You have a responsibility to work together with your wife. Even if she is in complete agreement with you, she deserves the chance to state her ideas and thoughts.

Any preacher who feels so insecure that he has to pressure his wife in order to make himself look good is cheating his congregation. Wives who complain, "My husband doesn't care about me, he cares about how I will come across to the church," probably have a legitimate complaint.

Brian Newman tells of a pastor's wife who was in a support group for children of alcoholics that met on Wednesday nights during church time. Her worried husband asked Brian, "What will the congregation think if my wife isn't here at church? They'll think she isn't supporting me."

Brian asked him, "Which do you think she would get the most out of, Wednesday night church or the support group?"

Without a moment's hesitation the pastor said, "The support group, of course. It's especially helping her with her eating problems."

Brian then asked, "If your first call is to love your wife as Christ loved the church, and if this group is so good for her, why is it a problem for you?"

The woman went to the group with her husband's blessing.

Dave Congo and his wife, Jan, actively appreciate and express the differences between the two of them. "When we present seminars in churches, we get up on the platform together and both talk to the group," Dave says. "The presentation goes back and forth between us with us interrupting each other, adding to what the other has said, offering thoughts and illustrations. Our aim is to demonstrate our partnership; we're in this together. Jan and I are very different, both in personality and in the way we express ourselves, yet God has used both of us as we operate as a team."

Relieving Your Wife's Stress

If you are communicating on a regular basis, your wife will be able to tell you the things that cause her stress, then

together you can come up with ways to work toward relieving it. Even when the stresses cannot be removed, you can
give your wife the emotional support she needs. Does the
church place unrealistic expectations on her? Stand up for
her to the congregation. (And be careful that you are not
contributing by piling on even more expectations.) Does she
feel lonely? Help her find ways to meet her need for friends.
Does she feel overwhelmed? Encourage her to step back
from specific involvements, then stand between her and
those who would criticize her for doing so.

You can lessen your wife's stress by taking care not to
"dump" on her. Use judgment in what you bring home
from the office to tell her. You may have had a horrible day,
but her shoulders are only so wide. It isn't fair to overload
her with every gripe you have about the staff. Certainly,
share with her, but do use judgment. Some of the sharing
may best be done with another pastor or a special Christian
friend. Don't tell your wife things that have been told you
in confidence or things that would reflect badly on someone
else, even if she asks you. If your wife can be part of the
solution, talk. If not, leave her out of it. If your wife continues to suffer from stress, it might be a good idea for her
to talk with a professional who can help her handle the
pressures in her life.

Linda Riley, herself a minister's wife, publishes *Serving
Together*, a free resource newsletter for ministry families.
She has also organized a group of volunteers who counsel
on "The Listening Line," a telephone hotline for pastors'
wives. Pastors' wives who need peer counseling, referrals,
prayer, or just a listening ear are invited to telephone.
Every volunteer who answers calls has at least ten years'
experience as a minister's wife as well as training as a lis-
tener. (This line, 1–213-214-2332, is open Monday through
Saturday, 10:00 A.M. to 4:00 P.M. Pacific Time. If the caller

cannot afford the long-distance charge, the hotline will accept collect calls.)

Many other resources are available for pastors and their spouses. Encourage your wife to make use of them.

Your wife is being called upon to fill one of the most challenging roles in our society. It takes courage for a woman to look objectively at her ministry situation, to find an approach that fits her and her family, and then to act appropriately and with perseverance. Whatever ministry style fits your wife, she can flourish best when she enjoys the privilege of having time alone with you, when you affirm her abilities and choices, when you stand behind her to encourage and support, and when your marriage is healthy and fulfilling.

7

Family Relationships

"When my daughter was in her late teens I asked her, 'Has it been tough being a preacher's kid?'" Dick Meier recalls. "I expected her to say, 'Oh, no, Dad, it's been fun!' Instead, for a long while she looked at me in silence. Then, with tears in her eyes, she said, 'Yes, Dad, it was hard. It was very hard.'"

Like pastors and their wives, the children of ministers are saddled with stereotypical prototypes and expectations too. "When people hear that my dad is a pastor, they either assume I'm a rebellious wild woman or a stuffy religious nut," said one teenage PK (preacher's kid).

"A lot of guys I wanted to date were afraid they weren't perfect enough to go out with the preacher's kid," Dick's daughter explained.

A minister's young son said, "Sometimes when kids find out what my father does, they say, 'Oh, is your dad like one of those guys on TV?'"

Expectations press in from all sides. Dick Meier once heard of a pastor who said to his children, "Your behavior is important because it could affect whether or not we stay on at this church." What a terrible thing to say to kids. How unfair of a father to put the security of his job on his children's shoulders. The truth was, that minister was looking out for his own interests, not theirs.

121

We've all heard the horror stories about pastors' kids and their problems. Without a doubt many members of the clergy have a great deal of trouble allowing their children to be human. From a very early age they put pressure on their kids to be perfect. Much of that goes back to the pastor's own insecurity. "The church is looking at me," he thinks. "If my kids turn out badly, they're going to think I'm a bad pastor and they'll get rid of me." Instead of putting the pressure on themselves, they lay it on their children.

Pastors are human, and they have a right to have children who are human. It's time for clergymen to stand together and say, "Hey, our kids aren't perfect, and that's okay."

How do you measure up in the area of family relationships? To help you determine, see how many of the following statements you can check.

_____ I spend time individually with each of my children.

_____ My family has special times reserved for family activities on a weekly basis.

_____ I make a real effort not to pile too many expectations on my children.

_____ I try to stay in touch with the issues confronting children and teenagers in my congregation and to understand the pressures my children are under.

_____ I make a conscious effort not to be overly worried about how people look at my children. Rather than striving to meet the expectations of others, I try to do what is best for my family.

_____ I am flexible when legitimate needs arise.

Don't feel bad if you weren't able to check all five statements as unequivocally true. Almost all of us need to work on our family relationships to one degree or another. And any positive change begins with becoming more realistic in our expectations.

First, you must forget perfection. That's right. You can have healthy family relationships even if your kids aren't perfect and even if you and your wife aren't perfect parents. Pretty good news, don't you think?

No More Super Family

Everyone, it seems, expects clergy couples to have model marriages. Other couples in the congregation can confess to marital problems—in fact, they may even be praised for their openness and honesty when they do. But if the minister acknowledges that he's having problems in his marriage, the congregation is likely to respond with disillusionment and judgment and question his spirituality.

An amazing number of kids grow up thinking their parents know nothing about failure because many parents don't share their failure experiences with their children. Many parents never discuss what it feels like to fail. This is especially true for clergy families who feel pressured to set a spiritual and moral example for the congregation. Churches want their ministers' spouses to be ideal wives and mothers, their children to be upright and godly. It's ironic that church members often criticize the pastor's children for the very behaviors they are unable to control in their own kids. When anyone in the pastor's family fails to meet the lofty standards set up for them, many churches respond by coming down hard.

When ministers' children react to such unrealistically

high expectations, it often shows itself in one of two ways: either they buy into those expectations or they rebel against them.

Those who adopt the unreasonable standards usually show a surprising "maturity" that Mom and Dad and the entire congregation encourage and reinforce. It all looks so great. But when the children grow up they mourn the childhood they never had. Playfulness? Joy? Spontaneity? All of these may be completely alien to them.

The rebellious preacher's kid is the common stereotype forced upon the children of ministers. One problem with stereotypes is that they tend to become self-fulfilling prophecies, which in turn seem to justify the stereotypes. Sooner or later virtually every minister's child will do something someone considers "unruly." Given such a no-win situation, some simply give up and "raise Cain"—just like everyone always said they would.

In a fairer world, the same things should be expected from clergy parents that are expected of any other parents: that they allow their kids to fail, that they not put undue pressure on them to be any particular way, that the kids not be held responsible for their parents' prestige and job security. Like any other kids, PKs have a right to resent having to do things just to make their parents look good to others. "They're not worried about me," said a teenage boy of his parents. "They're just worried about how I'll look to their friends and the church."

Pastor, don't demand that your family be a "super family." Talk about your failures to your children and help them see such times as opportunities for growth. If you have failed your children, you might say something like, "I've done the best I know how to do for you, but I've made mistakes. I've made a big mistake here and it has hurt you. I'm so sorry."

Carefully examine the expectations you lay on your children, and do all you can to shield your kids from the unrealistic expectations of others. Most of all, love your children, instruct them, pray for them, and respect each one of them for who he or she is.

Break Down Communication Blocks

Dr. Frank Minirth tells of a seventeen-year-old pastor's son who came to see him. "I was amazed at how strongly anti-Christian this boy was," Dr. Minirth recalls. "He was into sex, drugs, alcohol—all kinds of stuff." For a long time Dr. Minirth talked to the boy in an effort to discover some reason for his behavior.

Finally the boy said, "My father always preaches to me. He never just talks. With him it always has to be a sermon."

Preaching is what pastors do. When they preach, people listen and are challenged. It's what pastors are paid for. Unfortunately, some can't seem to communicate without preaching—not even within their own families. However good a preacher you are, home is no place for sermons.

So how does a preacher communicate without preaching? By listening, caring, sharing, and interacting. In Dick Meier's family, this included scheduled talk times together. Once a week they would go around the family circle and everyone would have a chance to share two things: a highlight of his or her week, and an account of the most stressful event (sometimes that stressful event was Dad, Dick recalls!). The person sharing could ask for family help and suggestions, or could simply say, "I'm working this out on my own." The only wrinkle was, if someone chose not to talk, he or she had to put money in the kitty. Talk or contribute, that was the choice. When there was enough money in the kitty, everyone would go out for a special treat.

After watching Mom and Dad share regularly in such a situation, it becomes much easier for the kids to get involved. That, in turn, allows parents to keep up to date with the kids—not so easy a task when the children become teenagers and begin to cast off their parents' convictions and put on their own. Weekly talk times will help you keep current with your kids' interests, with what turns them on and what turns them off. If you know what your young people like, you pretty much know them. If you know what causes them stress, you pretty much know their struggles.

When Dick's children were older, the family held council meetings. "Anyone in the family could call one," Dick says. "The ground rules were that I was the moderator, and I could veto anything I felt might threaten the welfare of the house or any member of the family. For instance, my daughter suggested we all take a vacation to Hawaii. Financially, that would have been a real threat to us, so over her protests I vetoed the idea." What Dick's approach did was to give the children a chance to be heard—and sometimes even to prevail. "My daughter loved pizza. I maintained it was just a conglomeration of junk that clogs up your insides," Dick says (although he admits he has changed his mind about that). "One of her favorite proposals was that instead of eating at the cheap steak place I liked, we would all go out for pizza. She could make her proposal and give all of its advantages, and I couldn't interrupt her until she gave up the floor (she had up to three minutes). Only then could I state my side. Then she could call for a vote. My son loved pizza too, and my wife is independent enough to ensure that I didn't always have it my way. We ate a lot of pizza during those years!"

When the pizza side would win yet again, Dick would put on an exaggerated disappointment act: "Oh, nuts! Not again! Do you have any idea what they put in that pizza? Ohhhhhh!"

His daughter would roll on the floor laughing and exclaiming, "We did it! We did it! We get pizza tonight!"

The major benefit to truly communicating with your family is that your kids know you care about them and their ideas. They feel respected, trusted, and important. An open forum allows all family members to bring up things they might otherwise be reluctant to mention, because now they have a chance of prevailing. "We talked about my getting my ears pierced at a family council," Lorraine Meier recalls. "Dick gave an impassioned plea against it and voted no. But when he was outvoted, he accepted it. If it hadn't been for family council, I don't think I ever would have brought the matter up."

There are other benefits to such a method of communication. "To this day my children are independent thinkers," Dick says. "They know how to present their side well and aren't afraid to speak up, yet they are willing to yield to the majority." And, for Dick, there was yet another side benefit—he has learned to like pizza!

To help prepare their children for what they might encounter later on, Dick and Lorraine would role-play with their children during family time. Dick says, "I'd ask them, 'What would you do if someone offered you marijuana and called you names if you refused?' I'd ask my daughter, 'What would you do if you were out on a date and the guy tried to get into heavy petting? What if it went too far?' The kids were not in those situations yet, but I figured when they got there they would be armed with some possible approaches."

Did you notice the question marks in Dick's conversation? He didn't *tell* his kids what to do, he *asked* them. If a child didn't have an answer—or sometimes even if he did—the rest of the family could share ideas and suggestions.

One thing about such open sharing is that you can't control—or always foresee—what a family member might say. (After all, the goal is to be honest and open.) Suppose you posed the marijuana question to your child and he were to answer, "I don't think there's anything that wrong with marijuana. I know it's a problem to you; but, hey, you lived so long ago you really don't know what life is like now. I think I'd try it, then I could decide whether I liked it or not." What would you do then?

Dick Meier suggests you try a little "verbal judo" and pull your child along rather than try to push back at him. You might ask, "Well, what are the advantages of trying it?"

"I'd be accepted by the other kids," he might say. "Everyone won't think I'm so out of it."

A good response would be, "Being accepted is a good thing. It feels awful to be out of it. But aren't there better ways to be accepted?"

Listen to your child's ideas; then, with his permission, share why you feel so uncomfortable with marijuana use: "I feel uncomfortable with that because of the health problems that go along with using marijuana. Despite what you may hear from your friends, a great majority of drug users say they started by smoking pot. Also, whether you agree with it or not, marijuana use is against the law." Then when you have stated your case, ask, "Does that make sense to you?"

In the end, your control over your children is limited to communication, especially as they grow older. But at least if you can communicate, you have a chance to convey your side of the issue. Beyond that, you can only hope and pray.

Slow the Racing Clock

"My husband had to spend the summer away on a mission trip," a pastor's wife told us. "While he was gone, people kept saying to our kids, 'I'll bet you miss your daddy, don't you?' One Sunday as we drove home from church, my daughter said, 'I don't know what to say when people ask if I miss Dad. I don't think it's all that much different from when he's home. We never see him anyway.'"

Another minister's wife said, "Our sons ask their father to play catch with them or to go fishing or to play a game of checkers, but he always says he has something to do at the church. On the rare occasions when he sits down to watch television or a video with them, he reads a book at the same time. I tell my husband that someday the boys will quit asking for his attention. He says he's really sorry but he just can't be everywhere at once."

It's the same in most pastors' families: the hardest problem to work around is the time factor.

"I have had to do a lot of things because my husband is gone so much," said a minister's wife from Chicago. "It would be easy to feel resentful." How does she handle it? "I have come to realize that every pastor's wife, regardless of her involvement at church, is in a team ministry with her husband. There are times when my husband ministers, and there are times when I minister. For the most part, my ministry is doing things to free him up so he can minister to the congregation. For example, I used to sing in the church choir. My husband would hurry home from the Wednesday night service to watch the kids while I went to practice. But it didn't work because he needed to stay around for the people who wanted to talk to him."

"I can't see ministry as a forty-hour-a-week job," said one minister, the father of three elementary school-aged children. "But then, who does work forty hours a week? I once worked as a jackhammer operator. I didn't get paid for the lunch hour nor for the two hours it took me to get to and from the job site. Altogether I was away from home a good eleven hours a day. Since we pastors expect other people to volunteer time to the church, we should expect the same of ourselves—perhaps five hours a week, what many spend who teach Sunday school classes. So to keep up with members of the congregation, I figure I should be devoting more like sixty hours a week to the church."

If you would allow it, you could be working in the ministry twenty-four hours a day. So how much time is enough? Forty hours a week? Sixty? More? There is no set answer. The important thing is to set your own boundaries, being sure to keep your priorities straight. Here are some of the suggestions offered by clergy families who are working at managing their own family time:

- Go out to breakfast or lunch together. If you stay home, people will call or stop by.

- Set aside specific times to be together (Tuesdays for lunch together or every other Monday night as your night out with your wife).

- Write out your schedules on a common family calendar. That way you know how your activities fit in with everyone else's.

- Determine that neither you nor your wife will be out more than three nights a week.

- Make it a point to all eat dinner together.

- Give your family permission to relinquish some of their church involvement.

- Set aside time for a family vacation. Whether it's a two week stretch or more frequent long weekends, schedule time for your family to get away together.

- Accept that part of your schedule that can't be changed or negotiated.

- Use creativity and discipline to make use of the moments you do have.

- Remind yourself of the positive side of your schedule. The flexibility allows you to go to school at 2:00 to watch Junior in his class play or to take your daughter to her 10:00 dentist appointment.

When your priorities are set, it's easier to weigh other demands on your time because you have already determined what's best for your family. Some invitations will have to be passed up. Some church meetings may have to be juggled. Certainly emergencies will come up, but you can feel better about responding to them because—with your priorities in place—you can feel assured that in the long haul it will balance out.

This is one of those important times for keeping your boundaries clear. When you make commitments and promises to your children, it is vital that you honor those commitments. If there is a true emergency that keeps you from fulfilling a promise (and *true* emergencies are fairly rare), explain it to your children and immediately make alternate plans with them as to when and how you will keep your original promise.

Adjusting to time demands is never easy for clergy families. You will always have scheduling conflicts. And accommodating the time crunch isn't always as pleasant as you might wish it to be. That's where planning and creativity and resourcefulness come in. If finding time for your family is important to you, you will do it.

Those Well-Placed Boundaries

A pastor we will call Mark Michaelson, a minister for more than twenty years, and his wife have a good, supportive marriage. Their two teenage boys are good kids, though not quite what is usually expected of a conservative pastor's family. Both boys sport wild haircuts and trendy clothes. Both also inherited their father's flamboyance, wit, and outgoing personality, and were outspoken at times.

Another pastor (we'll call him Ed Lee) was just the opposite. He told his son—a senior in high school—what clothes to wear, how to wear his hair, what he could and could not do, what time he had to be in at night. Ed's opinion was: "I don't have many more years to influence my son, so I've got to do what I can now. My best bet is to hold on tight and punish severely."

Certainly you need to set parameters for your children just as any concerned family would. But those parameters need to be ever widening. How else can your kids learn to make decisions for themselves and to accept the responsibility for them? How can they learn to be accountable?

Yet the fact is that your career could ultimately be affected by your children's behavior. If they go beyond the bottom line, there are consequences. That's why it is so important that you raise them to be responsible and to successfully move out of the nest. Suppressing children is not teaching them. By increasing their freedom as they grow and mature, and by guiding them to make correct decisions through the years, you are arming them for life.

Men in other professions would be aghast if their employers dared to make demands on their families. Yet this is precisely what happens in the families of ministers. It is up to you to set the boundaries for your own family. And it is important that you share your boundaries with the church. Only by talking can you and the church decide whether or not you can meet each other's expectations.

Even when the church doesn't actually interfere in the life of the minister's family, family members can suffer from psychological interference. This is the sense of not being appreciated as a separate person with the same rights to privacy and self-determination that are routinely accorded everyone else.

Must You Sacrifice Your Family?

Cathy, an anorexic young woman, came to us complaining of crippling insecurity. She gave a tearful account of her missionary parents sending her off to boarding school. "I cried and clung to my parents and pleaded, 'Please, please, don't make me go!' They told me to be good, that this was how it had to be for missionary kids." To this day Cathy is bitter and hurt and terribly resentful.

"My dad isn't really concerned about me," said an angry young man of his minister father. "He only cares about how I look to his friends and the church."

A middle-aged woman who was raised a PK feels the same. "I grew up with the feeling that I had better act in a very prescribed way because my actions were a reflection on my father's ministry. It was a terribly hard way to live."

Certainly appearances are important, but it's up to you to help your children see that you are not *just* concerned with how they look to others.

However they raise their children, wherever they set their boundaries, some pastors are going to end up in difficult situations because of their kids.

A pastor we'll call Dale Martin was shocked when his seventeen-year-old son Michael announced that his girlfriend was pregnant. Pastor Martin's response was to hold a Sunday evening love service of confession in which everyone in the congregation was invited to participate. Michael and Becky, his wife-to-be, agreed to be a part of the service. With tears streaming down his cheeks, Michael told the congregation how sorry he was. He said he had asked forgiveness from God and from Becky, and now he was asking for their forgiveness as well. No one doubted that he sincerely meant what he said. By service end, the tearful congregation was hugging and expressing their forgiveness. Rather than bringing on condemnation, the service pulled the church together.

"I appreciate the humility of Reverend Martin," Dick Meier says. "So many of us cannot admit to wrong in ourselves or in our families. Too many are defensive to the end, even if it means churches are pulled apart in the process." What power there is in humility! What strength in the willingness to admit you don't have all the answers.

Sometimes even the kids of the best of pastors get into trouble. When that happens, the goal should be to lead them back to a place of reconciliation and fellowship with the Lord. If your child has adopted a life-style contrary to what you can accept, it's important that you let him know: "These are the rules of our house. They apply to Mother and me, they apply to Uncle Joe and Aunt Sue, and they apply to you. We don't have illicit sex in this house, and we don't use drugs. You are welcome to live here only so long as your life fits within the parameters of what we stand for. Whatever you do, you will still be my child and I will love you. And, yes, you do have a right to make your own decisions and to do your own thing. But you can't do it here."

Just what your house rules will be is up to you and your

wife. Yours may be very different from those of another pastor or from the ones we have established for our families. What is important is that your children know what the rules are, and that they understand you will be consistent in enforcing those rules.

God never intended you to sacrifice your family for the ministry. Rather, He intends that the lives of those in your family be enriched just as you are enriching the lives of the families within your congregation.

Just Plain Families

Andy, the twelve-year-old son of a midwestern minister, was playing the lead in a local musical production. The director was a curt, demanding, inflexible woman. The year before, her close friend had died in a car accident, and she was angry at God for allowing it to happen. And because the minister's family knew God, she was angry at them by association.

Andy, never a terribly neat boy, had a habit of throwing his costumes down on the floor instead of hanging them up, and it made the director furious. One time some younger boys in the cast were pestering him and he told them to get out of his dressing room. When they didn't go, he pushed them out and one little fellow fell and skinned his knee. The director blew up, calling Andy names and cursing him and his family.

Of this situation Andy's father said, "We have never told our kids they have to adhere to a certain kind of behavior just because the people at church expect them to," the pastor said. "We won't let them do certain things, but that would be true even if I weren't the pastor. I had a long talk with Andy about the fact that a good part of the director's frustration with him was legitimate. He does need to be neat and pick up after himself. And he does need to be more Christian in his behavior with other kids even if they *are* bothering him. Andy needs to adhere to a certain level of behavior, not because he's the son of the pastor, but because he is a son of God.

"We are teaching Andy certain principles and values, not because we want him to parrot our views, but because we are convinced those values are sound. He also needs to learn that while people sometimes may not like him because he is a Christian, other times they may not like him because he's acting obnoxiously. It is important that he be able to recognize the difference."

The members of your congregation are fallible human beings. So are the members of your family. Your family has weaknesses just as others in your church have weaknesses. Your family has idiosyncrasies and unresolved issues just like everyone else does.

Basically, your family is not very different from other families around you. As individuals, you are subject to the same potentials and the same problems others face. You and your wife are not necessarily better parents than other adults, nor are you worse. And intrinsically, your children are just like any other kids.

The unfortunate fact is that many clergymen are much better prepared to minster to their congregations than to raise their children. Indeed, some preacher's kids insist that their fathers treat the church members with more patience and compassion than they do their own children. Just as some church members have superhuman expectations of clergymen and their families, pastors can fall into the trap of expecting their children to somehow avoid the normal slips and stumbles of growing up.

One minister's wife complained, "My husband expects so much of our teenager. He insists that our son not experience any of the temptations, mistakes, or failures that other young people go through. The boy has to be ultraspiritual and mature at all times. When he fails to live up to the unreasonably high standards set for him, his dad makes sure the boy knows he has failed and that he is disappointed in him. I'm afraid the time is coming when our son will quit trying."

Even in relatively healthy, average families, it is possible to produce codependent children if certain conditions exist. One of these harmful conditions is focusing on actions and behaviors rather than on attitudes and relationships. When we demand perfection from our children, when everything in the family seems to be based on and measured by performance, we run a high risk of developing children who will struggle with codependency for years to come, possibly for the rest of their lives.

How a pastor's kids look and behave is important, but only in the context of a family where relationships come first. Such a family will allow young people the freedom to grow, to make mistakes, and to fail. Only when these freedoms are present will there be room to develop a healthy and committed love. In the absence of these freedoms, rather than loving relationships there will only be bondage to endless measuring sticks.

When Dale Martin was confronted with the pregnancy of his son's girlfriend, before he went to the church body he called together the board members and told them about the problem. He said, "If even one of you feels this would be too much for the church and would cause it damage, I'll understand and turn in my resignation. But you need to know that my wife and I feel it's important that we stand beside our son and his wife-to-be."

He and the board members prayed together and cried together. In the end every one of them affirmed Pastor Martin's decision and vowed to stand behind him. One by one they said, "It could happen to any of us. Not a one of us is immune."

Families in Crisis

"My fifteen-year-old daughter was arrested for using drugs," a distraught pastor we shall call Robert Johnson told us. "Evidently, she's been doing it for over a year. I blame myself. I must not have done a very good job of raising her. Looking back, I see all kinds of places where I could have done better. I can't help envying my minister friends who have obviously been much more successful fathers than I. Their kids are doing great. I feel guilty, and at the same time I feel cheated."

When your family is endangered, everything else fades into the background. Your church, your minstry— everything that was so important yesterday suddenly loses its meaning.

When gripped by a crisis of their own, how can ministry families respond? The following suggestions come from the experiences of several families who have been there.

1. *Accept God's forgiveness.* God's forgiveness is available to your children, and it is available to you. This doesn't mean God will take away the consequences of mistakes or sins, but with forgiveness comes the opportunity for a new start. Whatever happened, it doesn't have to be the end.

2. *Share your feelings with your spouse.* Talk openly with her. Share your concerns, your fears, your anger, your guilt, and your hopes. Remember, she is suffering too. This is a time for closeness, not distance.

3. *Find an extended support system.* Talking with your wife will help a lot, but there will be times when you need to reach beyond to someone who is not so closely involved. Do you have a trusted friend to whom you can pour out your heart? Is there a minister friend with whom you might talk? Perhaps a competent Christian psychologist who would meet with you? A friend from a previous congregation or from seminary? Find someone you can trust, then pour out your hurt to him.

4. *Make use of the resources available.* Out of shame or embarrassment, the tendency for most of us is to hide our pain. But if you yield to this, it will cut you off from those who would offer you help and support, those who would pray with you and guide you to organizations that can assist you and your family. (The toll free number of the Minirth-Meier clinics is 1–800-545-1819.) Be willing to make yourself vulnerable, and be open to the resources that are available—including the secular ones.

5. *Lower your demands on yourself.* Don't expect to be as creative as usual, as objective or productive. Certainly keep on going, but understand that when you are enduring a long period of crisis, you may not be capable of giving your top performance. Give yourself permission to adjust your pace.

6. *Continue to hope and to expect things to improve.* Pray for faith. Read the Scriptures. Read the accounts of others who have been in a difficult place and yet have prevailed. Listen to the encouragements other people have to offer.

7. *Prepare for a happier future.* Though it may seem

impossible now, that better time will come. There
will be a day when you can work toward bringing
about positive changes, when you can assist in
someone else's healing. Determine that when that
time comes, you will be quick to comfort and slow
to judge, that you will be willing to sit with another in silence and offer advice only when it is requested. Vow that you will be available to
encourage and to affirm and to love. What a blessing you will be!

Three years after Pastor Johnson came to our clinic, he
called to tell us about a couple who had come to him after a
Sunday morning service. They were in such emotional pain
they could hardly speak. Eyes brimming with tears, the
man told him, "Pastor, our daughter has just been arrested
for dealing drugs. For three years we've reasoned and
pleaded and fought and prayed and cried with her, but
nothing has helped. As parents, we are terrible failures."

Pastor Johnson put his arm around the man's shoulders
and told him, "I have a daughter too, and I know exactly
how you feel."

"I used to blame God for allowing our daughter's problems," Pastor Johnson told us. "I don't anymore. I no longer
believe God caused our pain. But I do think He is providing
opportunities for us to use our experience to minister to
others in a way we never could have otherwise."

Keeping Your Family Healthy

Many of you are not in a crisis situation with your family.
Your concern is keeping your family as healthy as possible.
The following suggestions are for you.

1. *Determine to show affection to every member of your family every day.* Don't let a day go by without giving some individual attention to your wife and to each of your children. Put down the newspaper and listen when they want to tell you about their joys and their frustrations. Make an effort to understand their interests and concerns, and take them seriously when they share with you. Whatever is important to one of them should be important to you.

2. *Work toward building up the self-esteem of each person in your family.* Encourage each one's interests and abilities, even though they may not be yours. Listen to their problems, but don't be too quick to jump in with advice and solutions. In allowing them to develop their own problem-solving skills, you will be helping them feel capable and good about themselves.

3. *Talk and listen.* Talk about any changes or problems that are affecting your family. Explain how you feel about the situation, then be ready to listen quietly as family members tell how they feel. Let your children know they can ask you hard questions without feeling threatened. Try together to find constructive ways to deal with the problems. If the situations are serious, be willing to seek outside counseling.

4. *Provide an atmosphere of security for your children.* One way to do this is to establish family traditions and daily routines. The traditions may include such things as holiday activities, games you play together, weekends away. The daily activities

can include sharing the best and the most stressful events of the day, praying together, memorizing Scripture verses as a family.

5. *Recognize your limits and plan around them.* You don't have to be Super Dad. Your wife doesn't have to be Super Wife or Super Mom, and your kids don't have to be Super Kids. Encourage them to know their limits too, and help them plan around them.

6. *Hold weekly family meetings.* This will give you all a chance to discuss family activities, personal concerns, and family problems. Encourage everyone to speak, and insist that each one listen as well. Ridicule, sarcasm, and confrontation have no place in these family times.

7. *Pray for your family.* Ask God for His guidance and wisdom as you deal with your family day by day. Even in the most difficult or perplexing of times, you can find peace and comfort in the assurance of His loving care for all of you.

In healthy clergy families, much of the stress of life can be successfully handled. In many cases stresses can even be turned into positive experiences. One of the strongest predictors of whether or not your children will continue in the faith is the degree of emotional support they receive from you. Because few young people develop and mature spiritually on their own, it's important that you give serious consideration to how you might set aside the time and energy, and where you will set the boundaries, to best nurture your children.

One more thing. Don't underestimate the value of unconditional love. Demonstrate to each one of your children over and over and over again, "I love you for who you are, not for what you do." Dr. Rick Fowler tells of his daughter who is a gifted harpist. "She has plenty going for her, and she gets a lot of accolades from the community," he says. "The problem is that she begins to pick up acceptance by doing. If she doesn't do a thing well, she is sure she is a failure. Again and again I tell her, 'I don't care what you do or don't do. I love you just for who you are.'" How does Dr. Fowler's daughter respond? "Every time, without exception, she gives me a big hug and thanks me. She just can't seem to get enough of it."

Remember, too, that at different stages of life your family will have different needs. If you don't have children at home, for example, you can be freer to take on extra responsibilities. Understand and weigh the particular needs of your family right now.

The relationship you establish with your family will influence the relationship you will have with your church. The principles are the same: setting priorities, establishing boundaries, communicating, caring, loving, and learning to forgive. The end results can be far-reaching indeed, yet it all starts right here in your home.

8

Relationships within the Church

"If you ever find the perfect church, don't join it," the old saying goes. "If you do, you'll ruin its record."

Not new, perhaps, maybe not even profound, yet the old saw does contain a kernel of truth. That's the problem with churches; they are populated by imperfect people, people like you and me. It's not that Christians don't mean well; it's not that we aren't all working toward the same end; it's just that we are not perfect.

Your standing with God has to be the cornerstone upon which all other meaningful relationships are built, beginning with those within your own family. With such a foundation in place, you are ready to consider constructing relationships within the church: with the individuals, with the congregation as a whole, and with the governing board.

Your Relationship with Individuals

"A pastor has to really love the people," Dick Meier insists. "Pastoring is more than just another job, it's a ministry. He needs to pray for individuals, to think about them and their needs, to let them know in a personal way that he cares."

144

Some pastors are unable to echo those feelings. "The greatest frustration and irritation in my life is this church and the people in it," a minister announced from the pulpit one Sunday morning.

Pastor and people. What can you realistically expect of the relationship between you?

The truth of the ministry is that you and each of the people who attend your church are in this endeavor together. Public praise and private criticism, that is the way to develop a positive relationship with individuals. Let the people know you are behind them. "Every week, find some reason to praise someone publicly," Dick advises. "One Sunday, from the pulpit, you might acknowledge the nursery workers. Another Sunday you might recognize the ladies who bake cookies for children's church. Another week it might be teenagers who helped in a cleanup project. Look especially for those people who don't usually get public recognition." Praise, thanks, and appreciation on a personal level. They go a long, long way.

Your Relationship with the Congregation

It might be easier if you only had to relate to the people in your church on a one-to-one basis. Unfortunately, that's not how it works. A pastor also has to fit in with the entire church at large. What we're talking about here is pastor-church fit.

What happens, for instance, if a round pastor gets placed in a square church hole? He can function, he can move up and down and round and round, but there are all kinds of places where he won't really connect. While this certainly has to do with his particular personality, it is also affected by his own feelings about himself. If a pastor with low self-esteem is put into a job with high demands, he will be completely overwhelmed. On the other hand, if a pastor with a high sense of capabilities finds himself in a job with low demands, he will quickly become bored.

A man who came into the clinic to see us about his discontent with the ministry had served as the senior pastor in a large, prestigious church for more than ten years. Overworked and burned out, he had left the church and taken a job with a small rural congregation. But after pastoring the large church with all its activity and excitement and demands, he just couldn't muster the vision and heart for such a tiny ministry. There was no challenge left. "I can pastor this church with my little finger," he told us sadly.

Stress gets a lot of bad press these days. But the fact is, stress in itself isn't bad. It's what keeps us challenged; it's what gives meaning to our days. In working with pastors who are over-stressed and burning out, part of our goal is to find a pastor-church fit that provides just the right level of stress for that particular minister. It is when there is an extreme, either too much or too little stress, that problems start. Think of a master tuning the strings of his violin. At first, when just a little stress is applied to the strings, he can't even get a pitch, so he winds them tighter and tighter. But if too much stress is applied, the strings are going to snap.

Like the violin tuner, our goal is not to eliminate stress. It's to find the optimum level that will allow a pastor to be all he can be in the various areas of his ministry.

Your Relatonship with the Church Leaders . . .
in the Area of Finance

Finances cause many ministers a great deal of stress and anxiety. Low pay, guilt over "succumbing to materialism," the pressure of trying to make the church's financial ends meet—these are stresses that drag many pastors down.

Worthy of Your Hire

Who in his right mind would choose to enter the ministry strictly for the money? Probably no one. As a group, pastors are notoriously underpaid. Since in our society a man's salary symbolizes his worth and the respect due him, a church that pays its pastor adequately makes him feel worthwhile and appreciated. Fair compensation demonstrates the congregation's concern for their pastor and his family. To a frustrated clergy family who simply cannot afford to own a home, there is little comfort in the reminder that ministers are supposed to be above focusing on material concerns.

Many pastors struggle with the fact that every year they are a budget item. Their salaries are published and laid out for everyone to see. One pastor had this suggestion: "Next to the pictures in the church directory, why don't we list every family's annual salary? I mean, we're all equal, aren't we? If my salary is posted, why not everyone else's?"

If payday causes you stress, if you are frustrated about being undervalued, if you feel exposed whenever the budget comes out, do something about it. Speak to the board. Bring along an itemized list of your family's needs. Prepare salary comparisons, yours with those of pastors of similarly sized churches in your area.

Simply sitting by and harboring resentments will prevent you from having the strong, healthy relationship with your congregation that will benefit you both.

Church Finances

Have you ever been asked, "When I give money to the church, where does it go?" Not an unfair question, actually. Since your congregation is supporting the church, they have a right to see how their money is being spent.

Clearly and specifically, let the congregation know what the needs of the church are: "The sanctuary roof is leaking," "The youth group's room needs a carpet," "Our church library wants to purchase books that will minister to husbands and wives," "The Smith family is leaving for the mission field and needs moving expenses," "It's our church's turn to stock the local food pantry." Brian Newman tells of one Sunday in his church when all the chairs were taken out of the sanctuary and booths were set up to represent each of the places the church money went. "It was fabulous because people could see what they were supporting," he says. "Before that Sunday, I never knew we sent money to the children's home!"

Letting members see where their money goes helps them understand why they should contribute. That makes it easier for them to be "cheerful givers."

Spelling out the expenditures can also give a fresh perspective to you and your board members. In most cases, the church is way behind in recognizing and responding to the felt needs of the people. No wonder the New Age movement took the country by storm. It put workers out where the people were, ready to meet their personal needs in a practical way.

What part of your church's financial budget is dedicated to the physical and emotional needs of people? Certainly our mission is a spiritual one; yet the fact is, we cannot successfully talk to starving people about God until we first give them something to eat. The church of today needs to accept some responsibility for alleviating the hurts and needs in our society. Jesus said, "Inasmuch as you did it to one of the least of these My brethren, you did it to Me" (Matt. 25:40). Whether you sponsor groups for people with addiction problems, help for single parents, programs for divorce recovery, or whatever, meeting the felt needs of people is what will open the doors of your church to your community. A pretty sound investment, wouldn't you say?

Churches in Debt

"I don't like churches to be in debt," Dick Meier states. "It sets a bad example for members of the congregation."

Sounds like a great ideal, but with the financial realities of this day and age, how realistic is it? To a degree, that depends upon how generous and dependable church members are in their giving. That's why it's easy to become resentful toward people who don't put their money where their mouths are.

The following guidelines can help you keep your church debt free:

- Consider starting a building program only after your church can meet its budget on three offerings a month, leaving the fourth offering as surplus.

- Carefully weigh any pledge drive you might be considering to make certain no one is being intimidated into giving.

- Consider encouraging members of your congregation to make pledges without signing their names. This will give you an idea how much money you have to work with without running the risk of intimidating anyone.

- If God doesn't provide the money, perhaps the project shouldn't be done. Since He shows His will by opening some doors and closing others, consider this: Where the finger of the Lord points, the hand of the Lord provides. Be sure it's not *you* who has been doing the pointing.

Your Relationship as Leader

Whether you welcome it or not, your role as pastor firmly plants you in a unique place of leadership in the church. As a leader, what traits ought you to possess? Pose this question to any group of ministers, and you are sure to get a wide range of answers. We would like to suggest a few traits of a successful leader ourselves.

- *Leads with a gentle hand.* "Leader" is not to be confused with "boss." A pastor who is able to resist the temptation to legislate and order and lay down rules and pronounce ultimatums is the one who will be rewarded with the cooperation of those who look to him for guidance.

- *Is not afraid to get close to people.* "I was warned in seminary not to get close to people in the congregation or I would run the risk of losing my leadership," says Dick Meier. "For awhile I followed that advice, but I soon discovered how badly I needed people I could talk to. I needed friends. Finally I decided, 'This is silly. If being close to people causes me to lose my leadership, I must never really have had it in the first place.'"

- *Is willing to listen to others.* "As a pastor, I started out every week stopping in at the office of each of my staff members," Dick Meier recalls. "It wasn't anything formal. I'd just ask, 'How are things going?' This gave each person an opportunity to say whatever might be on his mind. My attention was on nothing but what that person had to say to me."

- *Welcomes feedback.* In their weekly meetings, Dick's staff would meet as a group to share ideas and seek solutions for any problems that may have come up through the week. Every pastor should put a priority on getting feedback from the other staff members. Without other viewpoints, a good deal of wisdom, insight, and objectivity will be missed.

  With the opportunity to have their views heard, staff members will be much more cooperative in working alongside you rather than against you.

- *Is in touch with everything that goes on at the church.* Supporting every person who works with you is an important part of leadership. Your staff members need to know you are behind them all the way. Here, too, praise and encouragement go far.

  "Our church had a Christian school," Dick recalls, "and the principal always attended our staff meetings. When he had a problem, the problem was everyone's. We talked over possible solutions and made sure he knew we supported him."

Because you are a leader, it's up to you to lead the church forward with wisdom, kindness, a listening ear, and a heart willing to learn.

Beware of the Quagmire of Legalism

As a leader, it's up to you to steer your congregation away from a rigidly legalistic stance. Rather than pulling a church together, legalism causes it to split apart at the seams. It overdoes the idea of controlling people's standards of right and wrong and their spirituality as Christians.

Some pastors have a long list of don'ts that never came from the mouth of God. "I know all about it," Dick Meier admits. "I was the king of legalism. I had rules for everything. My brother once came to talk to our church as a psychiatrist. When I saw he was wearing his hair partially over his ears, I took him into my office and said, 'I've got a real problem with your long hair, Paul. Can I cut it before you go out to talk to our people?' I cringe to remember it today, but right there in my office I gave my brother a haircut!

"The one who changed my legalistic course was a godly man who started coming to our church. He had a fine voice and wanted to sing in the choir. I looked at his longish hair and told him he'd have to get it cut. 'We want our men to be examples of manliness and spirituality to the boys,' I explained.

"The man answered, 'I understand your situation. But I wonder, do you have a verse of Scripture on this?'

"I admitted I didn't.

"'Well,' he said, 'I notice you have two or three people in the choir who are really obese. There *are* a couple of Scripture verses about gluttony. Do you have any problems with them singing in the choir?'

"I had to tell him, 'You got me!' It was then I realized I couldn't be everyone's policeman. I had to accept that there is liberty in Christ."

Certainly there are parameters. But in those areas to which Scripture doesn't speak, a successful leader will allow God's people to be led of the Holy Spirit.

Most pastors want the best for their congregations. They sincerely want every person to be all he or she can be. But while sincerity is important, it isn't everything. The Pharisees also started out sincere. Then they began to make rules with the idea that people would have to break the man-made rule before they broke scriptural rules. That way the people would be warned ahead of time. Pretty soon no one could tell which rules were from God and which were from the Pharisees. Yet the Pharisees kept right on adding to the list until they had more than six hundred rules the Scriptures never even mentioned. For their legalism, Jesus rebuked them soundly.

Yet legalism persists today. One minister preached against wearing open-toed shoes. When the deacons challenged him on it, the pastor was up in arms. Before long the church split. Another church split over the issue of women wearing slacks, even at home—"dressing like a man," some said accusingly. God's rules? Hardly. And, oh, so destructive.

It's wrong to pile heavy burdens onto each other that God Himself never laid on any of us. "To me, the scriptural admonition that my body is the temple of the Holy Spirit means that I shouldn't smoke," Dick Meier explains. "I have enough problems already without contracting lung cancer. But when one of my colleagues said that verse was why he doesn't drink coffee, I immediately bristled. 'Hey!' I told him, 'the Bible doesn't say anything about coffee!'"

We are living under grace, you and I and every other child of God. Leadership requires that a pastor study God's Word, that he be faithful in acting as he is led, and that he refrain from painting black or white the areas God has left open to choice.

Dissension

Conflicts and dissension are among the hardest things with which leaders have to deal. A leader cannot walk the fence indefinitely. If problems are not addressed, people become more and more dissatisfied, things start getting out of hand, and pretty soon people are leaving the church.

When conflict arises, you need to be able to look objectively at both sides of the issue; you need to be willing to follow your God-given convictions; and you need to act in whatever ways are necessary to bring about a solution. Gordon MacDonald said that in all criticism, we need to look for the nuggets of truth. A lot of what you hear may be exaggerated or confused or downright incorrect. Listen to both sides and try to extract the tiny nuggets of truth that undoubtedly are there. Then jump down off that fence and begin to actively work toward a solution.

Within the Denomination or Without?

Most ministers are associated with a specific denomination—some more happily than others. What can a pastor do when he begins to question the rules and doubt the beliefs on which his denomination has taken a stand?

Pastor Ron came to us saying he had decided to leave his strict, legalistic, rule-laden denomination. "We weren't even allowed to use musical instruments in our services," he explained. "I mean, there was no problem with the new church van, the dishwasher in the church kitchen, or the microphone at the pulpit; but because musical instruments weren't mentioned in the New Testament, we couldn't use them."

As Ron grew in the faith, he began to find more and more teachings that didn't seem to match the Bible. "I'm tired of all the extra-scriptural rules," he told us. "No wonder the younger people are leaving our churches in droves."

Because he dared to question and challenge areas of the church's thinking, Ron gained a reputation as a maverick.

Finally, after he was soundly reprimanded for saying he believed he would see Billy Graham in heaven, he began to think, *Things are* **really** *wrong here. I have to do something.* What Ron did was leave.

If you and your church have serious differences of opinion, you basically have four options: You can try to make changes from within; you can continue to compromise your convictions; you can determine people will just have to put up with your dissension; or, like Pastor Ron, you can leave that church. None of these decisions comes easily or without stress.

When It's Time to Leave

Very few pastors spend their entire ministry at one church. Sometimes the move to a new church is very positive; other times it is filled with pain. Whether happy or sad or somewhere in between, when it comes time to leave a church, it helps to first be reminded of something you already know: Ultimately God, who cares so much for you, is in charge. Supported by this comforting truth, get ready to take action. All the while, talk with others who can help you see things objectively. Whether another pastor, a counselor, or a good friend, it can be wonderfully healing to have someone with whom you can share your feelings.

When is the right time for a pastor to make a move? Not necessarily when trouble is present. Trouble comes and trouble goes. And not necessarily when the church attendance has leveled off. There are times of planting and there are times of reaping. Don't be too quick to bail out.

The time to leave is when a pastor is convinced his work at that church is through, when he feels he has taken the congregation as far as he can. This decision should be reached only after a good deal of prayer, a careful weighing of the pros and cons, and consultation with his wife and family.

"When I was facing the decision of whether or not to leave our church in Kansas to move here to Dallas to join the Minirth-Meier Clinic, Lorraine and I made out a pro/con sheet," says Dick Meier. "On one side we put down all the reasons why the move made sense: considerations about my health, the fact that my brother had been asking me for ten years to come and work with him, my training in counseling, and so forth. On the other side we put down all the reasons to stay put: the success we were seeing in the church, the good friends we had there, our 'Heaven's Angels' motorcycle group."

Their list in hand, Dick and Lorraine put into effect the following five-step plan for determining God's will.

1. *Ask yourself, What does the Bible say?* Was there anything scripturally pro or con, either about any of the items on their list or about moving to Dallas in general?

2. *Pray together about it once every day.* Point by point, Dick and Lorraine brought each item on their list before the Lord. They also asked God to bring other considerations, ones they had overlooked, to their minds.

3. *Seek wise counsel.* Dick and Lorraine talked to the doctor who was monitoring Dick's health. They asked a couple of pastor friends for counsel. They asked Dick's brother, who not only knew Dick and Lorraine but also many of their concerns, for his advice.

4. *Consider your circumstances.* The Meiers asked

themselves what was going on in their lives at that time. How was their health being affected by it? In what ways did their age affect the picture? What doors were open and which were closed?

During these first four steps, Dick and Lorraine added to and deleted from their pro/con list: "Here's something we didn't consider," one might say. "Now that I think about it, this doesn't make a lot of sense. Let's scratch it off," the other would add.

"A strong circumstantial pro was the selling of our house," Dick says. "We put it on the market on Friday, and the second person who looked at it—a couple who came early Saturday morning—wrote out a check for the entire amount we were asking. Talk about a circumstantial go-ahead!"

As time went on, the pro/con sheet began to lean more and more to the pro side. There were still some valid points on the con side, but the pro side was much longer and much stronger. Dick and Lorraine made the move.

"It was the right thing at the right time," Dick says. "Our congregation, which had grown to more than two thousand members, was in a neighborhood that was rapidly becoming industrialized and would have to relocate. That building program, and all the stresses that would go along with it, helped me see that this was a good time to pass on the baton."

Finally Dick and Lorraine proceeded to step number five.

5. *Wait for the peace of God.* This is more subjective and feeling-oriented than the other steps. The degree of peace people feel correlates to their personality type. A naturally calm person can easily look

at a decision he has made and feel calm and assured that he has done the right thing. "On the other hand," Dick admits, "I'm an anxious person, so making important decisions requires a major step of faith on my part and I still feel anxious. I have to rely on the first four steps and just go ahead with the decision. Usually I don't have the peace until afterward."

If at all possible, a pastor's children should be involved in such a decision. They should be able to pray too, and to add pros and cons of their own to the list. Certainly, it is hard for kids to move away from their friends; but on the positive side, a move presents them with the opportunity to experience the benefits of making new friends. But do carefully consider the wisdom of making a move during your child's teen years. At this age their network of friends is especially important.

If you do decide to leave, it is best to give your church a month's notice. The best approach is to start at the top, talking alone to a key person (such as the head deacon or elder). Next, tell the entire church board of your decision, and ask them to keep it confidential (although it seldom seems to happen that way!) so that you can be the one to announce your decision to the congregation. What this approach does is to show your respect for the leadership of the church.

If You Are Let Go

A pastor came to the clinic insisting he needed to see someone right away. "I'm going to be fired," he said in desperation. "The elders have given me one month to resign. But why should I step down? I haven't done anything wrong. My only crime is that I dared to cross a powerful family who has been running preachers out of that church for years. Well, I know I'm right on this, and I'm determined to stand my ground!"

After talking out the pros and cons of this unfortunate situation, the minister and his counselor came to the conclusion that he should resign rather than stay and be fired. Firing causes such devastation, not only for the pastor, but also for his wife and children. And the negative record makes it very difficult for him to get into another church.

A fifty-year-old pastor we will call Dan McVey was the hard-working minister of a large, downtown church. When the board voted to hire an associate, Pastor McVey was excited. With someone to help, he would be able to get started on several projects he felt strongly about but just never had the time to pursue. The new associate, who had spent twenty years in the business community, was especially knowledgeable in the very areas Pastor McVey considered himself weak. Before too many months had passed, however, it became clear things were not working out well. The new man scoffed at Pastor McVey's special projects. "Shortsighted," he called them. In fact, he was critical of the pastor's whole approach to the ministry: "Disorganized and narrow-minded," he stated publicly. Then one day in March, eight months after the new man had joined the staff, Dan McVey, senior pastor for thirty-five years, was fired.

Pastor McVey, shocked, hurt, and very angry, threatened to take the matter to court. In an effort to cope with the messy situation that was developing, he and his wife drove to Atlantic City for a few days of rest and relaxation. For the first time in his life, Dan McVey tried his hand at the gaming tables.

That summer, when Dan McVey left the church and the

city, he went from a high-salary position to an unemployment check, from a lovely church-owned home to an inexpensive apartment, from a prestigious church that showered him with accolades to disgrace. By now he was taking frequent day trips to Atlantic City: "Just to relieve the pressure," he assured his wife.

Six months later, still unemployed, Dan McVey offered his services for the summer to a sedate little church five hundred miles away. To add a bit of spice to his life, he would regularly go to a town about forty miles away where nobody knew him and play poker.

We first learned about Dan McVey when his wife telephoned us from her sister's house where she had gone for an extended visit. "He's got to get some help," she said in desperation. "I've been covering for his gambling too long. When people come to the house I tell them he's out making calls. But I'm not going to lie for him anymore." The final straw, she told us, had come when he failed to show up for a church wedding he was supposed to perform.

Without his wife to cover for him, Pastor McVey could no longer function. Early one Sunday morning, in agonized turmoil, he went to the chairman of the board of deacons and said, "I just can't preach today. You'll have to get somebody else."

By the time Dan McVey was brought to the clinic, he was devastated. "It's all over," he told us miserably. "I know the truth, yet here I am living a lie. The beginning of the end was getting fired."

It required intensive work and determination for Dan McVey to come to the place where he was once again a viable part of a ministry. Although his present church is a small one, he says, "It's vital and it's growing."

"Avoid getting fired at all costs," Dick Meier advises pastors. "Make every attempt to iron out the difficulties. As soon as you sense problems are brewing, take the initiative: talk one-to-one with the church board members, and be ready to listen with an open mind to what they have to say to you. If, despite all you do, you know the end is coming, then resign. Don't just sit still and wait."

Not only is it better for the preacher when he can leave gracefully, it's also far better for the church. Besides the pain and defensiveness a firing causes the congregation, the community is hurt. Communities have a tendency to develop attitudes toward a church the same way we develop attitudes toward individuals: "It's kind and gentle" or "It's cranky, fussy, and hard to please." It can take years for a church to get over such an event; many never do.

For his own good, a pastor who has been fired needs to seek counseling. He needs help in rebuilding his life. He might also enlist the aid of other ministers who will encourage and support him—older pastors who have seen the tough times, perhaps retired pastors who have so much wisdom to be tapped.

When You Come into a New Church

A wise minister will make sure he knows a church before he takes a position there. He will be sure he and the church fit together compatibly. If he accepts the position knowing what he's getting into, the adjustment will be easier for everyone. For instance, a pastor who comes into a church who loved their minister may be in for some painful adjustments. That church is going to have expectations; many people will have it in their heads that the way their former pastor did things is the only way those things can be done.

If there are changes to be made, make them slowly.

Don't approach the situation assuming you will "straighten the church out." Make an effort to fit in with the traditions of the congregation.

However carefully you evaluate the new church and the way it will fit you, conflicts can arise. If you have criticisms or complaints, should you speak about them to the board? That depends. Keep in mind that you only have so many trump cards in life. Once you have played them, they are gone. You need to decide which battles are really important to win, and which don't matter that much.

When a new minister comes to a church, people are usually open to some adjustment and change, but they aren't open to changing everything. It is vital that you decide where you will say, "We really need to change this" and where you can say, "I'm flexible. I can make some adjustments too."

With your cornerstone of a strong relationship with God firmly anchored, and your foundation of healthy relationships at home carefully laid, you are an approachable pastor. You are one who understands the value of strong, healthy relationships, one who models and encourages them in his church.

The next step is to look at you and your needs. Let's talk about shepherding the shepherd.

PART

IV

SHEPHERDING THE SHEPHERD

9

A Pastor's Job Description

Bakers bake, bankers bank, mail carriers carry the mail, musicians make music, ministers minister. The job description for a baker, a banker, a mail carrier, and a musician are pretty clear, but what exactly does a minister do? Just what is expected of a pastor?

To fill the job description of today's pastor sounds like a job for Superman. A pastor is expected to make house calls as willingly as yesterday's country doctor, to shake hands and smile like a politician on the campaign trail, to entertain like a stand-up comedian, to teach the Scriptures like a theology professor, and to counsel like a psychologist with the wisdom of Solomon. He should run the church like a top-level business executive, handle finances like a career accountant, and deal with the public like an expert diplomat at the United Nations. No wonder so many pastors are confused about just what is expected of them and how they will ever manage to live up to all those expectations. Many centuries ago, the prophet Micah tackled the question, "What does God expect of me?" God's basic job description for each of us is clear: "He has shown you, O man, what is good; / And what does the LORD require of you / But to do justly, / To love mercy, / And to walk humbly with your God?" (Mic. 6:8).

God requires that you who serve as pastors first and foremost know God. What you are is far more important than what you do. Not only do you have a responsibility to cultivate a godly life for your own sake, but you also do for the sake of the people to whom you minister as well as for society at large. You are God's front line.

A pastor must be a shepherd to the flock God has entrusted to him. He is to love and care for the people.

The minister must also stand before the people as a preacher. Indeed, teaching and warning and correcting and expounding Scripture are the central responsibilities of any minister of God.

A pastor must be in tune with the world around him. There is no room for ostrich ministers who bury their heads in the sand and refuse to see what they don't want to see. We live in a hurting world, just as Jesus did. And like Jesus, pastors have a responsibility to do what they can to speak out against the evils of society and to minister to the sufferings of mankind.

The minister's job description also includes overseer. Although administration is the bane of many pastors, and though it must never become a pastor's major work, the fact is that even in business matters the buck stops at the pastor's desk.

Gerald Kennedy, in his book *Fresh Every Morning*, plotted three separate approaches to the ministry. One is the pastor whose attitude says, "I am here for you to serve me." His congregation's reason for existence is to provide a stage for its talented pastor. Another approach is the pastor who willingly maintains, "I am here to serve you." His people often respond by making him their errand boy. A third approach is the minister who says to his congregation, "Come, let us serve Christ together." It is this pastor who understands what it means to oversee the ministry. Under his guidance, every person in the church can work together in the service of the Lord.

Although the specific job descriptions of pastors will vary greatly, as a minister you can expect to wear four separate hats: the preacher's hat, the shepherd's hat, the social worker's hat, and the businessman's hat. In addition to whatever hat you are wearing at a given time, you will always be expected to have on the mantle of consistent Christianity.

Tough? Absolutely. Demanding? You bet! Impossible? Not at all.

But let's start at the beginning. Before we look at what's waiting for you on your hat rack, let's examine your mantle.

The Mantle of Consistent Christianity

Although a consistent Christian life is something God demands of every one of His children, a pastor has a special responsibility in that his congregation, and society at large, is watching to see how he lives.

Health and Appearance

A pastor who is untidy in his personal appearance is not appealing to a congregation. In one national survey, 98 percent of the respondents stated that they would vote against calling a minister who was careless about his clothes and personal hygiene. Cleanliness may not be next to godliness, but it certainly makes a pastor more pleasant to be around.

As you look through the following suggestions, check any areas in which you might need some improvements.

_____ Do you keep yourself healthy and fit by eating right, exercising regularly, and getting enough rest?

_____ Do you keep your hair and nails neat and your clothes clean and pressed?

_____ Do you dress appropriately for each occasion?

Overall Decorum

From the day a pastor first arrives at a new church in a new community until the day he leaves, he is judged as a representative of God. People in the community are constantly listening to his words and watching his actions to see whether or not what he teaches and preaches is indeed a part of his life. Pastors have a singular responsibility to demonstrate Christ and to build up the church. It is an awesome charge. One careless slip in personal conduct, one thoughtless word, a momentary betrayal of a confidence can destroy in seconds what a pastor has spent years building. To better portray the living Christ in your daily life, consider the following questions. Check any areas you may need to strengthen.

_____ Do you make it a rule to always tell the truth and always keep your word?

_____ Do you guard every confidence committed to you? Are you careful not to tell even other staff members or your wife unless there is a real reason to do so?

_____ Do you obey the law—including when driving your car and when paying your taxes? Do you exercise self-control in every area of your life?

_____ Are you careful to keep your appointments? Do you show your respect for others by being on time?

_____ Are you honest, dependable, and faithful in your

financial dealings? (This includes paying your bills on time and living within your income.)

_____ Are you quick to point out people's strengths and slow to point out their weaknesses? Are you patient with others?

_____ Do you keep your anger under control?

_____ Remembering that all that many people ever see of Jesus is what they see in you, are you courteous, friendly, loving, and caring?

_____ Do you resist the temptation to demonstrate the depths of your knowledge, wisdom, and insight to everyone?

_____ Understanding that your opinions will not always be right, are you able to resist the temptation to be dogmatic?

_____ In dealing with others, do you try to put yourself in their shoes?

_____ Do you listen more than you talk?

_____ Are you careful to never be the bearer of gossip? Are you able to stamp out the gossip that comes to you?

_____ Is your sex life above reproach?

_____ Do you graciously accept whatever criticism is offered you and try to benefit from it?

Family Life

Because they are public figures, and because they are regarded as representatives of God, people watch the way pastors relate to their families. In fact, it is right there in his own family that a pastor faces his biggest test of whether or not he truly practices what he preaches.

We have talked a good deal about your relationship with your wife and children. To help you determine whether you have your priorities right, check any personal weakness you find when answering these questions.

_____ Are you faithful in honoring your vows to love and cherish your wife?

_____ Do you take an active and caring part in the life of your family, including participating in raising your children?

_____ Do you refuse to let others take over the time that belongs to your family?

_____ Do you love and accept your family members with all their imperfections?

_____ Do you understand that you need your home and your family as much as they need you?

Spiritual Life

Because most pastors are extremely conscientious, their tendency is to devote so much time to shepherding and nurturing others that they themselves go wanting. It is vital that a pastor understands that his own spiritual health directly affects his effectiveness as a minister. The time he allows for his own spiritual growth and nurturing is an investment in the people he pastors.

To promote your spiritual health and growth, check those areas in which you need to put a higher priority.

_____ Do you set aside quality time to spend alone with God—time for prayer, time for studying the Scriptures for no reason other than your own edification, and time for meditation?

_____ Do you allow scriptural truths to become real to you before you try to make them real to the congregation?

_____ Have you built one or two friendships in which you can allow yourself to be vulnerable and completely honest?

_____ Have you found another Christian to whom you can be accountable for your spiritual disciplines?

Now look back over the areas you checked. In each one, what specific actions might you take to make yourself a more effective pastor?

Problem Area   Specific Action

_____   _____
_____   _____
_____   _____
_____   _____
_____   _____

With your mantle of consistent Christianity firmly in place, you are now ready to don your various hats.

The Preacher Hat

During the French Revolution, when political prisoners were herded into dungeons, we are told of one man who managed to sneak in a Bible. The men crammed in with him longed to hear the Word of God, but the cell was so dark it was impossible to read. Once each day, for a few moments, a small shaft of light would come through a tiny window near the ceiling. So each day, at just the right time, the prisoners would lift the man with the Bible onto their shoulders and into the sunlight where he could read from the Scriptures. When the light was gone, they would bring the man down and anxiously implore, "Tell us, friend, what did you read while you were in the light?"

You, dear pastor, are like that man in the light. And those who sit in the pews before you are anxiously awaiting the insights and truths you have to share with them.

It has been said that there are no great preachers, only more responsible ones and less responsible ones. It is one of the wonders of the ministry that a pastor does not have to be a great orator, or even to be an engaging speaker, for the Lord to use him. A pastor's calling is to set out the truth of God. How it is received is up to the hearers' openness and the leading of the Holy Spirit.

Nevertheless, we will all attest to the fact that a good presentation is much more enjoyable than a weak one. If you lack a presenter's touch, take heart. A great deal of effective preaching depends on technique, and technique can be learned and sharpened and honed. The material you have to work with is, after all, the same—the Scriptures and insights of the Christian faith.

A conscientious pastor can do a good deal to improve his preaching. He can:

- enroll in public speaking classes through a local college or seminary.

- join a group such as Toastmasters where he can get feedback from listeners and other speech givers.

- read a textbook or watch a videotape on public speaking that will help him brush up on the fundamentals.

- read a book or take a refresher course in homiletics. (John Stott's *Between Two Worlds* is a good book to consider.)

- listen to taped sermons, taking careful note of the effectiveness of the preacher's form.

The diligent pastor continually evaluates his own preaching. A good way to do this is to wait a week or so after you've given the sermon, when it's easier to be more objective; then listen to it on tape. Pastors who are not too insecure or too afraid to take a risk even ask members of the congregation to offer evaluations and suggestions.

However good a pastor's presentation skills, it means little if he has nothing to say. It is imperative that a minister make time for study. Learn to carve out a significant section of each day for reading, studying, and preparing.

The Shepherd Hat

Although the importance of your preaching goes without question, the men and women who struggle under their burdens of hurts and needs also look to you for shepherding. After the most brilliant of sermons has faded from their minds, people will remember how their pastor cared for them.

For the pastor, shepherding is a demanding job, both time consuming and energy draining. For the congregation it is comforting, healing, and essential. When you wear your shepherding hat, you will be called upon to visit and to offer comfort.

Visiting

If you find it hard to visit, you are not alone. It's especially difficult if you do your calling in a hit-and-miss fashion. Try one of the following four systematic approaches, and see if it doesn't help both you and your congregation to get more out of your visiting hours.

1. *Make an effort to visit each family in your congregation once each year.* Set aside a certain month or season during which you will do your best to pay a short visit to each family. Then, during the rest of the year, restrict your visits to those with special needs.

2. *Determine how many visits you will make each week, then stick to your goal.* When possible, make appointments to make the best use of your time. If two of the people you had planned to see won't be home, fill in their spots with two other people.

3. *Set aside a certain time for calling.* If you determine that Tuesday afternoons and Thursday evenings will be your calling hours, then as much as possible limit your calls to those times.

4. *Lay out your church by geographical areas.* This will help you maximize your time and fuel.

Church attenders like to have a visit from their pastor. They appreciate knowing he cares enough about them to fit them into his busy schedule. The following suggestions will help you make the most of your visit.

- *Have a purpose for the visit.* Is there a special need

in the home? Have you missed seeing the family in church? Do you want to pray with them?

- *Set time limits.* Otherwise, it's easy to let the time get away from you. Not only will it be difficult for you to meet with other people who are expecting you, but you may end up intruding on plans the family had.

- *Make the family glad you came.* Show an interest in each person—mention such things as the children's school or special projects, birthdays or anniversaries, health or employment concerns. Anything that is important to someone in the family should be important to you.

- *When appropriate, read a few verses of Scripture and offer a brief prayer for the family.* Remember their specific concerns or problems they are facing.

- *Keep a record of the calls you make.* Jot down the date, any information about the family, and special needs on which you need to follow up.

- *Call ahead to make sure your visit will be at a convenient time for the family.* If there is still no one home, leave a brief note saying you were there and are sorry you missed them.

- *Consider options to visiting.* Sometimes a telephone call or a note or letter will be more helpful than a visit.

All people appreciate having a pastor who wants to get to know them. And it helps the pastor know where his congregation is coming from, where they hurt, and what their needs are.

Offering Comfort

When people are sick or sorrowing or dying, they have an especially urgent need to reach out to God. Tough times often make people more willing to consider spiritual truths. It is during times of tears that pastors are often able to point otherwise resistant men and women to God.

What can you do to minister effectively to those who are hurting?

You can visit the sick.

When you do, concentrate on the patient. Sit beside her and look her in the eye. Touch him. And though you should keep the visit short (unless there is a special need for more time), don't appear to be anxious to leave. Read a few appropriate verses of Scripture. Talk about God's love and His care and wisdom. Pray for the patient's comfort and possible healing and for God's grace. Most of all, if the patient needs to talk, be ready to listen.

Understand that in the sick room, you represent God. If you are calm and caring, if your trust in God is clear, if you demonstrate an expectant hope in God's wisdom and in the eternal future that awaits God's children, it will mean more than any words you could possibly speak.

You can comfort the sorrowing.

When you learn that someone in your congregation has died, contact the family immediately. If possible, go to them. As they struggle through their grief and cope with their loss, let them know you have not forgotten them. Encourage them to cry and to verbalize their anger, guilt, and grief. Gently lead them toward acceptance of their loss. See them for follow-up visits until their grief is resolved.

You can counsel the distressed.

You will be better equipped to meet the hurting people who come to you for counsel if you are acquainted with the realities of life. Read articles and books about situations that exist in our society. Attend presentations on such problems as domestic violence and drug addiction. Knowledge will help you understand, sympathize, and empathize. Another way to prepare yourself is to conduct a search for biblical answers and principles that will meet people's problems in a practical way.

Do all you can to be sure your shepherd hat fits as comfortably as possible. You will likely be donning it more often than any other.

The Social Worker Hat

"I want my congregation to be more involved in social issues," said the pastor of a large west-coast Presbyterian church. "I want them to take a stand on abortion, to speak out against pornography, to do more to champion the family. I want them to be less passively accepting of what the church has to offer and more actively involved in working toward the good of others. I want them to care."

This minister is in good company. In the *Christianity Today*/Gallup poll, three out of four of those questioned believe that religious organizations should take a public position on what they feel to be the will of God in political-economic matters. In impressive numbers, they also responded that "religious organizations should try to persuade senators and representatives to enact legislation they would like to see become law."[1]

Pastors do care, and they want their people to care too.

Author Haddon Robinson wrote in "A Profile of the American Clergy": "*Christianity Today*/Gallup poll and members of the press don't pose identical pictures of the American clergy. Ministers as a group hold much more conservative positions on theological and ethical questions than a newspaper reader might suspect. Nor do ministers live in steeples high above the pavement. In impressive numbers, they get involved at a personal level with needy men and women around them."[2]

Whatever your feelings about your social worker's hat, keep it handy. Our society badly needs ministers who not only care but are willing to speak out and take action for the betterment of society.

The Businessman Hat

If you are like most pastors, this is probably the hat you would most like to pack away in mothballs. If your church is fortunate enough to have a church administrator, you may think you can do exactly that. But do put it on long enough to take the important first step of asking for a written job description. It will let you know just what is expected of you.

Many ministers struggle with the challenge of overseeing the church staff. How is your staff management style? Look at the following ten statements and see how many are true of you.

_____ I create a climate of openness, mutual respect, and teamwork.

_____ I am completely clear about my expectations for each member of my staff.

_____ I put priorities on my expectations so that each staff member knows in what order tasks are to be completed.

_____ I specify the role each person is expected to fulfill and how that role fits into the church structure.

_____ I give each staff member the authority to do what is expected of him or her.

_____ I encourage each member to let me know what he or she needs to get the job done and then provide it.

_____ I express my specific appreciation for a job well done.

_____ I provide timely feedback, both positive and negative.

_____ I respect and work toward nurturing the self-worth of each individual.

_____ I discourage workaholism.

The more statements you were able to check, the more comfortable you can feel about the effectiveness of your management style. Look carefully at the those items you were not able to check, straighten your businessman's hat, and start today to improve yourself as a staff manager.

Preacher hat, shepherd hat, social worker hat, businessman hat—your job description as pastor will require that you wear them all.

10

The Morals Morass

F rank Tillapaugh and his exciting ideas for church outreach made a major impact on the Christian world. In his book *Unleashing the Church*, he described how he successfully reached people who would never have come to a traditional church building. One of his tactics was holding Sunday school in restaurants that weren't open on Sunday mornings. Before long, he was presenting seminars all over the country. Then the news broke: Frank Tillapaugh, successful pastor, author who influenced the thinking of so many Christians, had been having an affair with his secretary for ten years.[1]

The gallery of sincere Christians, well-known men who have done great things to forward the cause of Christ but then have sunken into the morals morass, could go on and on. You know about them. You've read the accounts in newspapers, you've seen them on the evening news, you've likely even had people point them out to you. And probably you, like the rest of us, are left with the nagging question: *Why?*

Brian Newman, who himself spent time in the ministry, says, "Pastors are under such extreme pressure. No wonder they are becoming more and more vulnerable to the sin of immorality. They counsel, they serve, they jam an enormous number of jobs into their days. Their parishioners look up to them and depend on them. Sometimes that dependency goes too far."

Certainly, for some pastors there are predisposing factors. According to Brian, many come from dysfunctional families. A good number suffer from workaholism. In addition, the wives of many middle-aged pastors were brought up in nice Christian homes where they were taught to be overly submissive, to support their husbands, and to be very involved in their ministries. Yet many of these wives complain that they get very little emotional support from their husbands.

Susan, a pastor's wife, came to us for treatment for her overeating. Yet when she started to talk, what she had to say wasn't about herself—it was about her husband. "He's a pastor," Susan told us, pain and anger dripping from her voice. "That's all. Pastor is his only identity." Everything the man gave, he gave to the church. As an example, Susan told of the family's recent ill-fated camping vacation. "We packed up our car and loaded up the kids, and finally drove away from the constantly ringing telephone. After driving all day, we unloaded the car and set up camp. Not an hour later my husband got a message that the eighty-two-year-old mother of a woman in our congregation had died. The woman didn't even attend our church—she was a member of a congregation down the street. Well, we packed up our car, rounded up the kids, and drove all the way back home so my husband could conduct the woman's funeral service."

Susan wept as she related story after story about how everybody came first except her. Wringing her handkerchief nervously, she said in little more than a whisper, "I think what's really happening is that he's seeing another woman. It's happening to lots of preachers these days."

Who's at Risk?

Sexual affairs don't hit out of the blue. They are the end result of underlying problems. And usually the signs of trouble are there long before the affair occurs, though often they aren't recognized as danger signals.

Certain steps lead almost predictably to affairs. Pastors who succumb usually have not developed behavioral guidelines for themselves, and for many their discretionary principles are weak. Discretion is personal judgment. It's a boundary line a person sets concerning the way in which he will behave toward the opposite sex. Because of denial, many young pastors don't realize how much potential really exists for any human to fall into an unexpected trap like an affair. The apostle Paul told us we are most likely to fall when we think we stand safe. We tend to underestimate our need for boundaries.

"For myself," Dick Meier says, "I have determined that I won't counsel a woman at night when no one is around. If there is an emergency, several of us will be there. I won't take any woman out alone to eat—maybe two or three, but not one. I won't send a card signed 'Dick'; whether my wife knows the woman or not, it will be signed 'Dick and Lorraine.' Those are some of my discretionary principles."

Have you set down discretionary principles for yourself? It is a wise thing for every pastor to do.

Dick Meier insists there are red flags to warn a person that he is becoming overly involved. In fact, there are five steps which lead almost inevitably to an affair.

1. Emotional Delight

For each of us, there are some people we just naturally like to be with. Chemistry, some call it. Of course, there's nothing wrong with enjoying another's company; but if that other person is a woman, this attraction should be a yellow flag of warning.

2. Extra Time Together

The second step is spending extra time with the person who provides the emotional delight. Nothing improper is taking place here; the two are just hanging around a little longer after a committee meeting or getting together to plan a class or volunteering to work together on a project.

Although the time spent together may be perfectly legitimate, what the person is doing is feeding on point number one because it feels so good. Seeking this time together is a warning that probably some areas in the pastor's marriage need attention. A bit of a vacuum is there. It is time to step back and do some serious checking.

Or the pastor's marriage may be excellent, but he may have some love-hungers from childhood pains he suffered from parental absence or abuse. "All pastors, just like all Christian therapists, should receive some personal therapy before doing therapy for others," says Dr. Paul Meier.

3. Excessive Touching

Now the red flag is definitely up. Rather than greeting with a handshake, it's a direct hug, maybe a lingering one. It might be a massage to soothe a sore neck or a comforting caress of the back. There is always an innocent reason for the hug or massage or caress, but what it boils down to is simply an excuse to touch. Touching leads to more touching, then to more, then more. Now that red flag is waving hard and fast.

4. Secret Rendezvous

"Let's meet together for breakfast," the two may decide. Or "Let's take a break and go for a walk." Usually the destination is some out-of-the-way place where the two can hold hands, talk about their problems, and comfort each other. Now they are really on dangerous ground, for bonding between them is taking place.

5. Eromania

At this point the two are past the red-flag stage. When this "addictive craziness" sets in, there is such an infatuation that no one can come between them. If someone warns, "Don't you think this is a little dangerous?" the defensive answer is "Get off my back! I know what I'm doing." By this stage the two are so committed, it's almost like drug addicts needing a fix; they are going to proceed no matter what. Unless God intervenes and wakes them up, an affair is almost inevitable. It's like a toboggan that has already started sliding downhill. You can put your feet out and drag it, but you can't stop it.

Watching a pastor in this stage is like watching a man drinking poison. You give him all the reasons he should stop. While acknowledging his needs and difficulties, you try to point out in a nonjudgmental way that there are better ways to handle those problems, you give him all the logical arguments about the risk to his family and career. But in the end, you can do nothing but stand by and watch him drink the poison down.

"I've had pastors in this last stage come in to talk about their situation," Dick says. "Although I warn them to be rational and objective, they insist on being emotional: 'We need each other.' 'I can minister to her.' 'God brought us together.' "

"Two people don't ever have an affair with each other because of genuine love," says Dr. Paul Meier. "It may seem that way to their denial systems; but in reality, they both feel inferior and are selfishly using each other to cause themselves to seem more significant."

In the end the pastor loses everything—his church, his family, his witness. His wife, struggling to understand what happened, ends up blaming herself. But it isn't her fault. Even if there were problems in the marriage, there is never an excuse for an affair.

"I firmly believe that the Holy Spirit warns the individual at every step," Dick says. "He says, 'Look at what you're doing. There's still time to stop.' If he gets caught up in an affair, a minister has no one to blame but himself."

Life Boundaries

When we are not able to effectively set boundaries for ourselves, we are apt to ultimately lose control of our lives.

A nationally known minister we will call Dr. James pastored a huge church that sported a brand new building and an amphitheater-type sanctuary. "Dynamic" is the best description of that church.

Dr. James built his ministry on charisma and visibility. When he entered the sanctuary on Sunday morning, he was always accompanied by an entourage. An excellent and captivating speaker, Dr. James cut a wonderfully attractive figure in the pulpit. Little wonder he had such a huge following.

Dr. Allen Doran attended Dr. James's church. "As a psychiatrist, I was really intrigued by him," Dr. Doran says.

The pastor wasn't accessible to the congregation, however. In fact, the church developed a counseling center mainly to serve as a buffer to help protect him.

Dr. James was especially careful to guard his time with his family. He was resolutely unreachable by anyone on Tuesdays, his family day. He talked about it in his sermons, though not as much as he talked about their family vacations. Dr. Doran recalls, "The vacation I remember best was a two-week canoe trip they took. I could just picture them there—a nice-looking man, a very attractive wife, beautiful children—everyone's idea of the all-American family.

"I greatly admired the man," Dr. Doran says. "He was intelligent, he was a wonderfully skilled orator, he seemed to have everything figured out. But there was that one thing. While he seemed so outgoing and gregarious in public, alone he was different, sort of like the actor who is a laugh a minute on stage, but by himself is quiet and shy."

Dr. James didn't speak extemporaneously. His sermons were prepared to the word and rehearsed until they were almost memorized. Yet he held one evening service a month where people were allowed to ask him anything they wanted to. "A curious format for a man like Dr. James," Dr. Doran thought. And sure enough, as people fired out questions, it soon became clear that Dr. James was not going to answer anything he didn't want to answer. He was wonderfully adept at talking around issues. Without a doubt, any bridges between him and the congregation were not going to be easily crossed.

There was, however, an inner group, and with them things were different. Together they were something like a business corporation—just Dr. James surrounded by his tight-knit board of directors. No one else in church was privy to their inner workings. Imagine the shock when it came out that Dr. James was involved in an affair. The congregation, shaken to its foundation, couldn't believe it. "Not him," they said. "He's not that kind of person."

What kind of person was Dr. James? He was a man with precise, inflexible boundaries and great rigidity. He was a man who portrayed himself the way people wanted to see him. Yet he was also a man who loved God, a man who cared deeply about his church.

"Such tight boundaries and great rigidity can be a real problem," Dr. Doran says. "For such pastors, every issue becomes solidly black or solidly white surrounded by boundaries that absolutely cannot be crossed. If pressures become too great, pressing in from too many different directions, some of these pastors who have been so rigid in their boundaries are far more susceptible to transgressions than those who might be more flexible. We see this in psychiatry all the time. Allowing people to understand themselves and become more comfortable with a boundary that's an area rather than a thin line is ultimately a far better approach."

Being able to interact with boundaries better equips pastors to handle pressures and makes it less likely that they will rush in and make destructive decisions.

The Rationalization Defense

Some pastors reading this will see themselves and say, "Yes, but it's different in my case because . . .

. . . God wants us to be happy." (Where do you find that in the Bible?)

. . . I have to follow my feelings." (Feelings are not the voice of God.)

. . . I can witness better to her." (Why should she listen to what you have to say?)

Al Capone once said, "I've spent my whole life giving, and all I've received in return is abuse." The man who in many people's opinion was the number one criminal of all time had rationalized to where he could stand up, hold his head high, and claim he had done nothing wrong.

To one degree or another, we all rationalize. Simply put, rationalization is a subconscious defense whereby we make sinful, inappropriate behavior seem all right. It keeps us from seeing what we need to see. No wonder rationalization is so hard to overcome.

If you are called upon to minister to someone who is rationalizing his immoral behavior, the following steps might help.

1. *Start with an alliance with that person.* Accept the fact that you cannot win him over logically to what he doesn't want to see. The matter isn't open to logic. To persist in trying to reason with him will merely slam the door shut on any further communication on the subject.

2. *Get him to talk to you.* Invite him to tell you about what is going on. No matter how violently you disagree, listen to what he has to say.

3. *Give him feedback—cautiously. Cautiously* is the key word here. Don't preach, don't pontificate, don't lecture. It's best if you get others to give feed-

back as well, a "group therapy" type approach. He may pay more heed to several voices than he will to one.

Your efforts to convince the rationalizing person may or may not be successful. Some people will never see what they don't want to see. They will continue to rationalize for the rest of their lives. Most ministers, however, really do want to work through their problems.

An exceptionally well-educated pastor came to us after it was discovered that he was molesting his daughter. It was the devastated girl who had turned him in. As we talked, the pastor steadfastly rationalized his behavior with verses of Scripture. He dug up a passage out of the Old Testament he claimed would back up his actions since what he had done was "all right with the family." No matter what anyone else said, that man could not see any problem.

Finally we got him into group therapy. For a few days he only shared in general ways. Then he was pointedly asked, "Why are you here?"

As soon as the man told the group about his "activity" with his daughter, they cut loose on him. Several ladies in the group who had themselves been molested ganged up and really took him apart.

The first day the pastor resisted everything they said. The second day he was still rationalizing his actions. Finally, on the third day, the group began to get through to him that he *was* rationalizing, and that what he was doing was very, very wrong. By the end of our sessions together, the change in both the pastor's attitude and his behavior were astounding. When he could no longer rationalize, everything changed. He became overwhelmed with true guilt, and it took a great deal of therapy to help him overcome his depression when he finally saw the truth.

Affair-Proofing Your Marriage

Many surveys have been conducted to determine just how widespread adultery is in our society. The most reliable ones seem to indicate that approximately 40 percent of all married men and 35 percent of married women will seek sexual gratification outside their marriages. The reasons for affairs vary. "He never paid any attention to me," one might say. Another will state that "She didn't really care for me, so it wasn't a real marriage anyway" or "We've grown apart" or "God brought someone else to me."

A more appropriate question than *why* is, is there any way to make a marriage affair-proof? The following steps will go a long way toward protecting the sanctity of a marriage.

Share Regularly on a Personal Level

"She doesn't understand me" is the classic complaint of a cheating spouse. As human beings, we all want to be encouraged and nurtured and supported. And we want to feel close to someone who cares for us. When a marriage does not include these elements, a partner can easily feel starved for someone who will just accept him for who he is, someone who will talk pleasantly with him, someone who will care and comfort and praise and appreciate him.

The first thing a couple can do to prevent such desperation in each other is to keep each other up to date on their feelings, needs, concerns, and ideas. They can agree to set aside time just for that purpose (a good example is Dick and Lorraine Meier's talk dates).

It also helps to pray for each other. One approach is to have each partner write down three requests about him or herself. Then the couple can exchange lists, each committing to pray for the other's requests once a day.

The goal is to stay intimately attuned to each other's lives.

Confront Problems Before They Grow

No marriage is without its difficulties. People misunderstand, they are impatient, they take each other for granted. When it happens, the natural response is to get angry. The question is not "How can we eliminate difficulties?" but "How will we respond to them when they arise?" The easy way is to avoid confronting them, but the end result of such avoidance is that the problems multiply and grow until they drown us. The more difficult but healthier way is to deal with problems regularly and get them behind us.

Refuse to Control Each Other

Each partner thinks he or she has the greater understanding of good and bad and right and wrong. And most of us have many years of practice at our particular style of control: stubbornness, manipulation, intimidation, pouting, accusing, condescension. Although we may succeed at getting our way and justifying our position, what we don't seem to realize is the toll it takes on our marriage. The more one partner controls, the more the other chafes to shake loose.

The more control tactics are minimized, the more room there is for understanding and trust and acceptance.

Associate with Friends Who Build Up Your Marriage

Whether we admit it or not, we are inevitably influenced by the company we keep. Proverbs 13:20 tells us: "He who walks with wise men will be wise, / But the companion of fools will be destroyed." We talk about being independent and making up our own minds, but ultimately we take on the traits and attitudes of those we associate with most closely.

By forming our closest attachments with other Christian couples who have their priorities in line, our own values and commitment to God and to our partners are reinforced and strengthened.

Resources

The following materials can be of help to couples who want to strengthen their marriages.

- *Building Your Mate's Self-Esteem*, Dennis Rainey. This book for both husband and wife includes projects on which the couple can work. A great way to boost each other!

- *Courtship after Marriage*, Zig Ziglar. The author presents a six-step process to building and keeping romantic commitment in marriage.

- *Marriage before Divorce*, David Kilgore. This excellent book includes a monthlong project for couples to work on together. As partners work through it, they will find out a great deal about themselves and their relationship.

- *The Marriage Builder*, Lawrence Crabb, Jr. Integrating the spiritual, relational, and physical aspects of a couple's life is the central theme of this book.

- *The Marriage Track*, Claudia and Dave Arp. This workbook for couples will help them strengthen and build their marriage relationship using methods the authors have shared in their "Marriage Alive" workshops for more than fifteen years.

- *Passages of Marriage*, Dr. Frank and Mary Alice Minirth, et al. The five growth stages described in this book will take a couple's marriage on to greater intimacy and fulfillment.

- *The Secret of Staying in Love*, John Powell. Besides thought-provoking questions, this excellent book contains a list of helpful emotions for couples.

- *Sex in the Christian Marriage*, Meier, Meier, Minirth, Meier. This book focuses on revitalizing and rekindling the flame in established marriages.

Forgiveness and Restoration

An older pastor, struggling with an insatiable attraction to pornography, came to our clinic for help. "I liked him immediately," Dr. Frank Minirth says. "And I assured him right off, 'You're going to get better.'"

Dr. Minirth gave the man some suggestions and encouragements, then he said, "You know, I don't think the pornography is what's really bothering you. It seems to me that you are really sad."

At that, the old gentleman burst into tears. He talked about how he'd been hurt as a child, about the problems he was having with his own kids, of an affair he had had years before, of the problems his church was facing. He told about all the crises of his life, past and present, admitting his fault and asking God's forgiveness. And through it all he cried and grieved. There was no doubt about this man's sincerity. The amazing thing was that as the pastor talked and cried, and as Dr. Minirth supported and encouraged him, the pornography issue began to fade further and further into the background.

Such is the power of confession and forgiveness.

Is restoration really possible for a pastor who has succumbed to the temptations of the flesh? It was for pastor and author Gordon MacDonald. During his two-year restoration process, MacDonald was supported by his "seven angels," godly men across the country who nurtured, mentored, and counseled him, and to whom he was accountable. At the end of the two years, a restoration service was held for Gordon MacDonald in which he was reordained into the ministry.

When a preacher falls and truly wants to recover, he needs to first confess his sin to God. Then he needs to confess it to a counselor or to an older pastor—some other person to whom he can become accountable. He also needs to confess it to his wife.

But confession alone is not enough. The pastor also needs to amputate that third party. There must be total removal, even if it means leaving the church or the area. If he's involved with his secretary, either she has to go or he does. Maybe they both do (but not together!). It doesn't work to simply say, "We'll cut off the romantic relationship but continue our business relationship." The emotions run too deep. The bonding is too solidly set.

How does one cut ties without causing still greater pain to the one with whom he has been involved? "I usually have a person write a letter to the third party apologizing for leading her on," Dick Meier says. "I suggest he say, 'I've got to get you out of my life and be committed to my wife. You may need counseling, but I can't be your counselor. We must have no contact with each other, not even phone calls.' Then I ask him to let his wife read the letter and approve it."

Why a letter rather than a telephone call? Because a letter provides emotional distance—there's no immediate personal contact with that other person.

As for the pastor's future with the church, it depends. Denominational guidelines differ. Speaking as a former pastor himself, Dick Meier feels that such a pastor should resign, at least for a couple of years. During that time he should be getting counseling, personal as well as marriage. Then if he feels he wants to get back into the ministry, he should first spend a year or so on the staff of a church, working under some godly pastor to whom he would be accountable, in order to rebuild his stability and reputation.

After recovering from an affair, a pastor's counseling would need to be done within very specific and strict parameters.

If his wife agrees to keep their marriage intact, it is up to the husband to rebuild trust between them. If he is going to be home late, for instance, he needs to call and tell her where he is, why he will be late, and when she can expect him. Some men argue, "Why should I do that? She's not my mama." No, she isn't, but it is imperative that you rebuild that trust. It is your personal responsibility.

For the recovering pastor and his wife, joint counseling is a must. If he gets no help, it may well be just a matter of time until he is involved with someone else. His crisis and restoration will not alone close the need that caused the problem in the first place.

And If It Is the Wife Who Strayed?

More and more frequently, it is the pastor's wife who has had the affair. The common rationalization is, "My husband was married to the church. He had nothing left over for me. I only have so many years left in this life, and I don't want to live them this way." Somebody came along who was kind and sympathetic. "He met my needs," she insists, "and we can really relate to each other. I feel like a new person blossoming on the inside." Though a rationalization, the complaint within it is certainly valid. And indeed, her needs are perhaps being met by the other man, but this is the wrong way to go about having her needs met.

That's how it was with Darlene. She had several affairs. During the last one, her husband discovered her and the other man in bed together. The pastor left the ministry, his wife ran off with the other man, and the pastor and his wife were divorced. In his denomination, a divorced man—even if he was clearly the innocent party—could never again pastor a church. It's a sad ending, because this man was such a good pastor. "I was too wrapped up in my large church," he admits sadly. "I lost my sense of priorities."

While many men think they can get their needs met through achievement, most women realize the need to get theirs met through a relationship. If that isn't happening, a wife should talk to her husband. She should share her unmet needs and feelings of loneliness with him and ask that they have some serious discussions on options for restoring their relationship and nurturing one another. If he doesn't respond, then she should seek guidance from a Christian counselor.

When a pastor falls into the morals morass, all of Christendom suffers. Yet when repentance, forgiveness, and restoration prevail, the power of God shines through for all to see. Before this can happen, the pastor needs help and care for himself.

And to whom can the pastor turn for help and advice? Who will care for the caregiver? We're glad you asked, for that's exactly the subject of the next chapter.

11

Who Will Care for the Pastor?

I t would be hard to find a pastor who can't relate some casualty from among his peers. The fact is that Christian leaders do struggle.

What pastor hasn't wished he had someone to talk to when he didn't feel like being a pastor, someone to confide in when things at home were strained? "But," you may be asking, "how open can I really be? Is it fair for me to unload on someone else? If I share too much, will I be a stumbling block to others? Will my problems and struggles end up backfiring on me and on the ministry God gave me?"

Obviously, a minister cannot risk discussing highly personal problems with a member of the church. Nor is it necessarily safe to share with someone within the denomination. Nothing is more intimidating than the possibility that someone might use information shared in confidence as a weapon to hurt you or to damage your ministry. The sad fact is that many pastors who come to our clinic have no one to whom they can talk and still feel accepted.

Who Can You Call?

"When people have a problem, I suggest they talk first to God," Frank Minirth says. "You can be completely open with Him—He knows all about it anyway. Next, I suggest finding a peer—a Christian friend who is accepting and kind, who will give feedback but not from a demeaning position. Choose this person with great care; be certain it is someone who will be discreet. Third, I suggest someone professional. It may be a pastor, a Christian counselor, or even a Christian medical doctor."

Dr. Minirth's suggestions hold as true for the pastor whose wife needs help as for the one who needs help for himself.

Some other ideas come from fellow pastors.

"My friends from seminary are pastoring in different parts of the country," the pastor of an independent church in Maine told us. "I can call them and share with them and discuss my problems. It's very comfortable, because we aren't in competition with each other."

"I have a retired pastor I like to talk with," said the minister of a Reformed church in Colorado. "He's been in my shoes, he has great wisdom, he has time for me, and he appreciates me appreciating him. It's a good relationship for both of us."

"My closest confidant is another Christian minister who is about as opposite me theologically as he can be," said the pastor of a Methodist church. "We meet for breakfast once a week and just enjoy each other. We share and comfort and commiserate and, when asked, offer a word of advice. We don't talk theology, we talk like friends."

"One of my parishioners is a psychiatrist," said a pastor from Alabama. "He is also a good friend. I can't tell you how many times I have bent his ear and asked his advice."

If you don't have someone with whom you can share, put a high priority on finding the right person. You might want to follow the ideas of these pastors, or you might have an idea of your own. Either way, be sure the person you choose is someone you can trust to keep your confidence.

Why Share at All?

Dr. Charles Shepson, director of Fairhaven Ministries, a Tennessee center specializing in counseling for ministers, suggests the following as the leading reasons why "church workers" seek professional help: Depression (13 percent); marital problems (11 percent); extramarital affairs (8 percent); problems with authority (8 percent); and burnout (7 percent). "Forced terminations" and "conflict with parishioners" also made the list.

Especially in times of stress and crisis, ministers need to care for themselves, and they need to surround themselves with others who will help them do it. They need others to listen to their frustrations and to hear their ideas. For us humans, friendships are a vital part of growth, and pastors—like the rest of us—continually need to grow.

Burnout

The result of bearing pressure and strain so intense that they consume our inner resources is that last-ditch condition we know as burnout. (See pages 201–202 for a comparison of the burnout life-style with the balanced life-style.) Unfortunately, burnout doesn't get better by being ignored or denied. And it's no disgrace, either. Dr. Herbert Freudenberger calls burnout "a problem of good intentions." He states that, for the most part, people who fall prey to this condition are decent people who have worked hard to reach an admirable goal. Their schedules are chock-full, yet whatever the job, they can be counted on to do more than their share. They are the leaders who have never been able to accept limitations. They are those who have pushed themselves too hard for too long.

Responses to Life's Stressors[1]

<table>
<tr><td></td><td colspan="2">Leads to
Burnout</td><td>Leads to
Balance</td></tr>
<tr>
<td>F
E
E
L
I
N
G</td>
<td>Fatigue
Helplessness
Worthlessness
Hopelessness
Confusion</td>
<td>Bitterness
Worry
Panic
Boredom
Obsessiveness</td>
<td>Hope
Challenge
Competence
Personal significance
Self-control</td>
</tr>
<tr>
<td>P
H
Y
S
I
O
L
O
G
I
C
A
L</td>
<td colspan="2">Heightened muscle
  tension
High blood
  pressure
Faster heart rate
Shortness of breath
Headaches
Nausea
Hypertension
Heart disease
Memory problems
Sleep disorders</td>
<td>Improved physical health
Resistance to disease
Improved mental health
Resistance to future stressors</td>
</tr>
<tr>
<td>C
O
M
M
O
N

B
E
H
A
V
I
O
R
S</td>
<td colspan="2">Procrastination
Inactivity and
  paralysis
Indecision
Angry outbursts
Withdrawal
Cynicism
Interpersonal strife
Unassertiveness
Sleep disturbances
Overeating
Excess drinking
  and drug use
Weight loss
Memory losses
Daydreaming
Workaholism</td>
<td>Affirm self-worth
Activate forgiveness
Acknowledge God's sovereignty
Rethink purpose
Consider options
Set goals prayerfully and visualize
  their attainment
Begin to take action steps
Spot-check projects
Involve others
Awareness of one's pace
Accomplish goals
Recognize need for meditation
Exercise programs
Daily devotions
Practice relaxation techniques
Maintain intimate relationships
Take breaks
Celebrate new growth</td>
</tr>
</table>

	THINKING	
	God doesn't care	God and I are a great team
	I'm a failure	This is a challenge to be faced
	I think I'm sick	I am capable
	I can't think	There is hope
	I'm the only one who has gone through this	I can overcome this
	There's no way out	This stress can turn my life in a positive direction
	There's only one way out	What resources are available to me?
	If only . . .	What are my options?
	My past controls me	I am valuable and competent
	I always fail	What can I change in the future?
	I can't do anything right	I tried and I learned
	God won't forgive me	I learned things that didn't work
	I can't forgive myself	This is a temporary inconvenience
	Poor me	It's not the end
	Nobody likes me	Change is to be expected
	I need everyone's love and approval	Just trying makes me a winner
	I should be able to do everything well	
	I should worry	
	It's easier to avoid difficult things	
	Perfect solutions should be found for everything	
	It is right to feel bad	

	RESULTS	
	Dissatisfaction	Fulfillment
	High anxiety	Reduced anxiety
	Decreased productivity	Increased productivity
	Insecurity	Newly discovered security
	Intimate relationships suffer	Increased intimacy

Dr. Freudenberger suggests that burnout often affects those in the helping professions, people who sincerely want to make an impact on the lives of those around them. Yet people in such professions are the ones who are most likely to be called upon to share the pain and discouragement of others. They soon find that caring too much hurts too bad.

A person suffering from burnout, Dr. Freudenberger writes, is "someone in a state of fatigue or frustration brought about by devotion to a cause, way of life, or relationship that failed to produce the expected reward." This causes friction to build up deep inside, which inevitably depletes one's resources and robs one of his vitality, energy, and finally the ability to function.[2]

Going for Help

Friends, family, and colleagues can go a long way toward relieving stress and providing a listening ear, but there are times when that's not enough. Sometimes it is necessary to seek professional help.

Many sincere Christians are put off by the terms *psychologist* and *psychiatrist*. Those titles even make many pastors nervous. "I should be able to handle this problem myself," they say. "God and me—together we can get through anything. If I just pray a little more." Dr. Frank Minirth recalls a pastor who told him, "When I first started talking to you, I had a real poor opinion of psychiatrists. In fact, I thought psychiatry was just a hoax—nothing to offer people and definitely against the Bible. I told my congregation they should have nothing to do with it. Now I realize that some problems really can have a medical component, and that God can use knowledge outside of Scripture."

That pastor is right. God can use knowledge outside of Scripture so long as we are careful never to elevate that knowledge to the level of Scripture. It makes sense. We build skyscrapers even though the Bible doesn't tell us how. We fly in airplanes, though not even the basic concept of aerodynamics can be found in Scripture. We treat pneumonia with penicillin though its use occurs nowhere in the Bible. There is nothing wrong with making use of the knowledge in the world as long as we are careful to first put it through the grid of Scripture; certainly, any knowledge we use should be consistent with what we read in the Word of God.

When a person needs professional help, a Christian psychologist or psychiatrist may well be the best choice. Sometimes a professional just needs to be a friend to a pastor in crisis. A well-known evangelist came to Dr. Minirth and said, "I'm embarrassed to tell you this, but I have a lot of questions about my salvation. I think about it all the time and it worries me."

"Let me share with you some things you already know," Dr. Minirth told the evangelist. "You know Christ loves you. You know you don't have to be perfect for Him to accept you. You know His salvation is open to you."

After that initial meeting, Dr. Minirth met with the man about once a week, and each time he would tell the evangelist the same thing. "Even though he knew it as well as I, every time I'd give him these assurances it was like a shot in the arm to him," Dr. Minirth recalls. "And each time he needed to hear it once again."

Dr. Minirth assured the evangelist, "Many, many pastors have doubts. I have them myself. You aren't alone. It just seems worse to you because of the insecurities you are carrying around, but we can deal with that."

And deal with it they did. The evangelist got better and went back to the ministry. "All I did," says Dr. Minirth, "is tell him what he already knew. He just needed to hear it from someone else. The problem was, his parents had not given him that assurance of unconditional acceptance while he was growing up."

A very exciting area of help for pastors is the new ministries that are being developed by counseling pastors and retired pastors. (See Resources section at the end of this chapter.) The idea is to make use of the knowledge, wisdom, and experience of those who have been there and understand exactly where pastors are coming from.

A possibility for long-term rebuilding or recovery is to seek out a retired pastor you respect who would be willing to serve as a mentor to you. If he's in your church, that old question of "How much dare I reveal?" may creep in. Consider the question, but be careful that your caution doesn't become a defensive excuse for keeping your distance. Actually, many pastors find retired ministers less threatening than other possible support people—there is no competition between them, no stigma attached to seeing them, no concern that they don't really know what it's like. As for the retired ministers themselves, many would welcome the opportunity to share their wisdom and insights and to bring someone else along.

Encourage your denomination to set up a list of retired denominational pastors in the area and to make that list available to local pastors. Another idea might be to call your denominational headquarters and ask for the names and telephone numbers of retired pastors in the area; then prepare a list yourself and circulate it among other minsters who might be interested.

Of course, a mentor doesn't have to be retired. An older pastor in your area could act as one. A dear man who pastors in a small town in Alaska has as his assistant a very young pastor he is mentoring and who is preparing to take the church over when he retires. "Up there it's awfully hard to get pastors, especially good ones," the pastor explains. Mentoring can be a very rewarding experience for young pastors just starting out and also for the older pastors they assist, men who are overworked but serving in churches that cannot support another pastor.

To some degree, a pastor can also be mentored through a person's writings. Read books on the struggles other pastors have experienced, and discover how they came through. Read biographies or autobiographies of great preachers. See what they did right and what they did wrong. At the end of his life, Billy Sunday, the great baseball player turned even greater preacher, said, "I saved the world but I sent my own family to hell." A sobering thought from a remarkable Christian pastor who knew what it was like down there in the trenches.

Resources

The following resources can be of help to pastors. Explore them and discover what they might do for you.

Barnabas Ministries
Post Office Box 37179
Omaha, Nebraska 68137
(402) 895–5107
Pastors who are facing personal difficulties or problems within their ministries are the target for this group. The aim of Barnabas is to help pastors strengthen themselves, their ministries, and the life and programs of their churches through personal counseling and encouragement, support groups, workshops, and seminars.

Center for Continuing Education
Episcopal Theological Seminary in Virginia
Alexandria, Virginia 22304
(703) 370–6600

This six-week renewal and growth program is offered for members of the clergy three times a year. It provides that special opportunity to come apart from the demands and pressures of the ministry—and of life in general—for a period of reflection, learning, discovery, and coming to terms with your faith.

Fairhaven Ministries
Route 2, Box 1022
Roan Mountain, Tennessee 37687
(615) 542-5332

In 1989, 1,800 Christian leaders came to this retreat and vacation center for counseling—some just for rest and relaxation—and the program seems to grow each year. One important aspect of Fairhaven Ministries is that qualified counselors are available upon request.

Kettering Clergy Care Center
1259 East Dorothy Lane
Kettering, Ohio 45419
(513) 299-5288

This center offers professional care and support to pastors, missionaries, church leaders, and employees of church organizations and their families. Their services include counseling, crisis-intervention weekends, prevention of clergy burnout, enrichment for clergy marriages, and premarital and marital assessment programs. Kettering Clergy Care Center also offers a two-week residential clergy training and renewal experience.

Life Enrichment
14581 East Tufts Avenue
Aurora, Colorado 80015
(303) 693-3954

This organization seeks to strengthen Christian leaders in their relationships at home, in the ministry, and even in their leisure. How do they do it? In three ways:

1. Biblical counseling of the hurting leader, spouse, and family at no fee,

2. Consulting with the senior leader, board, and staff to strengthen the working relationships between them and to clarify their vision, and

3. Providing places of rest—and programs to go with them—and refreshment for the pastor and his wife.

Marble Retreat Center
Louis McBurney, M.D., and Melissa McBurney
139 Bannockburn
Marble, Colorado 81623

This interdenominational center ministers to pastors and their spouses. Up to four couples come for two weeks of individual and group counseling, which is equivalent to six months of conventional weekly counseling.

Paraklesis Ministries
161 Ottawa, NW, Suite 500
Grand Rapids, Michigan 49503
(616) 458-6759 or (800) 421-8352

This ministry helps pastors and their spouses grow spiritually, emotionally, and physically, as well as develop healthy relationships through counseling, seminars, consultations, and week-long retreats. It also provides training for church staffs and gives specific help for "pastors in crisis."

Son Scape Ministries
Post Office Box 7777
Pagosa Springs, Colorado 81147
(303) 264–4777

A place of rest, privacy, creative input, and spiritual retreat, Son Scape Ministries is situated in the San Juan Mountains of southern Colorado. It offers opportunities for personal sharing and counsel about the possible danger areas of the ministry.

Vallecito Pastoral Counseling
19731 County Road 501
Bayfield, Colorado 81122
(303) 884–2678

Counseling, career assessment, guidance, and consultation for ministers and their families can be found at this counseling center, located in southwestern Colorado. Therapy and marriage and family counseling is available for such issues as forced resignation, stress, and burnout.

And, of course, the Minirth-Meier clinics throughout America have a variety of therapies available for pastors, including inpatient and outpatient hospital programs. Call 1–800–545–1819 for more information about these.

Who will care for the pastor? Many are willing and able to do so. But first, the pastor must be willing to take care of himself. We will be discussing exactly that in the next chapter.

PART

V

LEADERS, STRONG AND TRUE

12

Toward Health and Wholeness

T he problem with so many studies on stress in the ministry is that they are too limited, either by region or by denomination.

"Well, sure, that may be true in California, but not here," pastors in the south might say of a study done out west.

Of a study conducted by the Catholic church, protestant ministers claim, "That's a problem Catholic priests have, not protestant ministers."

Dave Congo, determined to cross those barriers and gather more generalized information, designed a study that encompassed thirty-two different denominations, both protestant and Catholic, in thirty-eight states. His findings are especially meaningful because they are pulled from a cross section of ministers—pastors like you.

One of the most interesting findings from Dave Congo's survey was that there are two critical periods during which pastors tend to experience the most burnout: The first is during the first five years of ministry. "Because they are just starting out, their abilities tend to be lower than the demands from the church," Dave explains. The second is after fifteen years of ministry. Says Dave, "After fifteen years, the challenge is gone. The pastor has done it all so many times that he is getting bored. It's just not fun anymore."

Both of these situations tie in with the church's expectations of its pastor, and of the expectations the pastor puts on himself.

"This isn't what I envisioned when I was in seminary," said one young pastor who had just passed his one-year anniversary with his first church. "I had such hopes and dreams and goals. We were going to make a real impact, God and me. Now I'm out here where I can see what it's really like, and it's so much less than I expected."

"I've been a pastor for twenty-two years," said an overweight, graying forty-seven year old. "I look around at my church and hear the same old questions, see the same old difficulties and battles, and I can't help but ask myself, 'What difference is my life really making?'"

Do you see a part of yourself anywhere in these pictures? The lofty, sometimes unrealistic, ideals of the pastor just starting out? The weariness and lack of challenge of the experienced pastor? Or perhaps something else is preventing you from experiencing the joy God desires for you as you serve in partnership with Him. Whatever it is, let us share with you four steps toward a renewed health and wholeness in your ministry.

Step One: Affirm Your Partnership with God

Would you consider yourself basically problem-centered or mostly God-centered? Do you focus mainly on the problems, or are you able to raise your vision above them to the heavenly resources available to you? The difference between these two approaches is very significant.

Certainly, it makes no sense to try to push your problems into a closet and pretend they don't exist. There is no solution in denial. Problems do exist, and they need to be identified and faced head-on. But when we come to the place where we are operating in partnership with God, a good bit of the pressure of those problems—and the anxiety that surrounds them—is relieved.

After running for his life from his angry brother, Jacob finally fell down exhausted and used a stone for a pillow. God came to him that night in a dream, with angels traversing a ladder extended to the earth. When he awoke, Jacob said, "The LORD is in this place, and I did not know it" (Gen. 28:16). So often that's how it is with us. Wrapped up in dealing with day-to-day problems, struggling desperately to sort through everything and focus appropriately, it's easy to forget that God is in this place and that He is part of the solution. If God is living within us, He is closer to us than even those problems that so heavily beset us. His power and His strength and His resources are within our easy reach.

Dave Congo tells of his son who had a very large birthmark on his leg. When the boy was seven years old, Dave's wife Jan noticed that the eight-inch mole seemed to be changing color. She took the boy to a doctor who took one look at the spot and said, "Your child has got a melanoma." Immediately surgery was scheduled for early the next week.

"It was like someone had hit me in the stomach," Dave says. "My little son, my child who was just learning to read, just learning to throw a ball . . . I couldn't even think the rest." Dave and Jan walked out of the doctor's office in silence, consumed by their thoughts: *It isn't fair! He's just a little boy. He's so innocent. Why should he have cancer when he's only seven years old? He hasn't even had a chance to live yet. It just isn't right!* "It was so overwhelming," Dave recalls. "All I could feel was anxiety and hurt and confusion."

Dave and Jan were in a small prayer group at the time,

216 / What They Didn't Teach You in Seminary

and some dear, caring people gathered around them and encouraged and supported them. "We want to be with you in this," one man said. Then he added, "God is bigger than even *this* problem."

"That wasn't something Jan and I could say at that time," Dave admits. "We were struggling too hard just to keep our heads above water."

It is so important that we bring our concerns before the Lord. He is, after all, on our side. And He is with us. But even when we don't realize it, even when the pain and terror are so overwhelming we cannot pray, we *are* in partnership with God, and we *are* in His plan.

Dave and Jan's friends prayed and prayed. By the date of the surgery, the spot seemed to have diminished somewhat. When the surgeon removed it, no traces of cancer could be found. Was cancer ever there? "We really don't know," Dave says, "but we do know it's not there now."

When crippling problems and tragedies occur, we become so problem-centered that our vision stops right there at the problem. It is at that very time we most need to refocus on God and who He is.

The problem may be your own or it may be someone else's. Either way, God is your partner and you can release the concern to Him. For instance, on your way home from the hospital where you have spent time comforting someone, you might pray, "I've done all I can, Lord. I can't do any more about Mary at this time, and I need some time to separate myself from this. I'm entrusting her now to your hands and am trusting you to care for her until I see her again."

Dave tells of a pastor friend who envisions himself packing all the cares and problems of the day into a knapsack he carries on his back. "When I get to the stop sign just before my house, I visualize myself taking that knapsack off and hanging it on the stop sign," the friends says. "Then I say, 'Okay, Lord, I'll leave it here for tonight. Tomorrow morning I'll pick it up and take it with me again.'"

If you are to be healthy and whole, you need to rest. You need to allow yourself time away from the ministry. God Himself modeled this idea of stepping away: For six days He worked, but on the seventh day He rested. It will be very difficult for you to separate yourself and rest unless you feel you are in partnership with someone who can take over. Here, then, is your challenge: Do what is possible, then turn over the impossible to your heavenly partner.

Step Two: Accept a Realistic Picture of Yourself

"A traveling evangelist once came to our church," Dick Meier recalls. "He told me he wanted to give the congregation an opportunity to show their appreciation to their pastor—me. 'The last time I was in a church this size,' he said, 'they gave their pastor a new car.' My eyes glazed over. My old clunker really was on its last legs."

The evangelist presented the opportunity, and the church responded heartily—with a wall clock for the pastor's office!

"It was a nice clock," Dick says. "I had been wanting one, and if my expectations hadn't been so high, I would have been thankful and loved it."

When you look at yourself in your pastor role, what do you see? Very few of us are good at seeing ourselves realistically. While some pastors do cast themselves in an overly positive light, far more see themselves too critically. We look at the wall clock and, because it isn't a new car, determine we have failed.

There are pastors who appear to be superhuman, ones with an incredible talent for being personable and making others feel understood. They have wonderfully impressive communication skills, and the ability to generate great warmth to those around them. When you see one of them, you will notice the special way he has about him that makes you feel you are the most accepted person around, that he has been thinking about you all day long. You know the kind of pastor I mean.

Intimidating, you say? The type of minister who makes your own efforts seem mundane and unimportant? Instead of being too quick to judge yourself against another minister, build a realistic picture of who you are. In the personal qualities bank below, check those that best describe you.

_____ achiever	_____ creative	_____ persuader
_____ action oriented	_____ dedicated	_____ practical
_____ affirmer	_____ independent	_____ promoter
_____ appraiser	_____ intelligent	_____ result-oriented
_____ attractive	_____ interdependent	_____ secure
_____ comforter	_____ leader	_____ sociable
_____ conventional	_____ motivator	_____ structured
_____ cooperative	_____ objective thinker	_____ teacher
_____ counselor	_____ organized	_____ team worker

Just look at how much you have going for you! Now let's go one step further by examining two more areas.

My five greatest strengths are:

1. _____
2. _____
3. _____
4. _____
5. _____

My five greatest weaknesses are:

1. _____
2. _____
3. _____
4. _____
5. _____

See yourself realistically. No, you are not a perfect person, but no one expects that of you. You cannot do everything, nor does God ask you to. You are who and what He made you to be. Accept that, thank God for it, and get busy using what He has given you.

Step Three: Use Positive Self-Talk

"I call myself a recovering perfectionist," says Dick Meier.

Rather than leave his work at the office at the end of the day and turn his attention to his family, he would bring his concerns home with him. Even as he was climbing into bed at night, he would still be worrying. "I don't know what I'm going to do about that deacon," he'd say to Lorraine. Or, "The woman who came in today has a real problem. I should have done more to help her." Lorraine would respond with a kind but firm, "So what?"

"She was right," Dick says. "So what? There was nothing I could do about it then. And it certainly wasn't the end of the world. Now Lorraine's words are built into my self-talk. I could have done this better? 'So what? I did the best I could at the time.' I wasn't able to find an answer for someone today? 'So what? There's always tomorrow.'"

What do you need to put into your own self-talk? What is

it in your own internal computer that needs to be reprogrammed?

Some pastors deal with the setbacks in their ministries by saying, "I'm a failure, I'm a failure, I'm a failure" until failure becomes their self-talk. Soon it is a self-fulfilling prophecy.

Have you struggled with failure, either in your ministry or in your personal life? Dr. Frank Minirth suggests eight steps for overcoming failure.

1. *Understand what failure really is.* Is it possible that your expectations are too high? Are you buying into the world's idea of success and failure rather than God's? Are you measuring your accomplishments against someone else's?

    When you do fail to meet your goals, understand that this doesn't mean that *you* are a failure. The difference between the two is the difference between merely failing at something and taking on the crippling attitude that "I'm no good."

2. *Realize that you're not alone.* Even if your failure is true failure, you're not alone. Many of the most successful and godly men who ever lived went through times of miserable failure. Consider Moses who couldn't even talk right, Gideon who was the least of the least, David who committed adultery, Peter who denied Jesus three times. So you've failed? Welcome aboard! You've got plenty of company.

3. *Many issues we consider failures can later become strengths.* Consider 2 Corinthians 12:10, where Paul writes: "Therefore I take pleasure in infirmities, in reproaches, in needs, in persecutions, in dis-

tresses, for Christ's sake. For when I am weak, then I am strong." It is in our weaknesses that Christ can best demonstrate His power. Today's failure can become tomorrow's strength.

4. *Failure may give me the negative feedback I need to change.* When I have a goal I'm working toward, I look for feedback on my progress. If that feedback is negative, I know I had better make changes if I am ever to get back on course. Although the negative may be hard to hear and even harder to accept, I can learn from it what I could never learn from the positive.

5. *Realize that failure is a part of success.* You always hear about Babe Ruth's 714 home runs. What you don't hear about is the 1,330 times he struck out on his way to all those home runs. An old Japanese proverb says: "Fall seven times, stand up eight." Failure is a part of success.

6. *Each failure is of value.* As we fail, we learn. We grow a little and understand a bit better how to become more Christlike. Brian Newman tells the story of a businessman who made a million-dollar mistake and promptly wrote out his letter of resignation and took it to the president of the company.

"Why are you resigning?" the president asked.

"Well, in light of the million-dollar mistake I made, I figured you'd want me to leave," the businessman said.

"That was a million-dollar lesson," the president replied. "Now you're too valuable for us to get rid of."

7. *Failure is an opportunity for growth.* "One of my favorite verses says, 'The fruit of the Spirit is love, joy, peace, longsuffering, kindness, goodness, faithfulness, gentleness, self-control. Against such there is no law' (Gal. 5:22–23). Many times when I fail, I find it is a good chance for Christ to remind me that I have another opportunity to become more Christlike, to grow more patient, more self-controlled, more longsuffering, and so forth."

8. *Take failure with a sense of humor.* This is especially true where you find you are being perfectionistic. It helps to stand back and laugh at your own failures and problems.

Instead of allowing your self-talk to pull you down, use it to raise you up. Consider this paraphrase of 1 Corinthians 4:3–4: "I care very little if I am judged by you . . . I do not even judge myself. My conscience is clear. It is the Lord who judges me." This gives you four wonderful phrases to use in your positive self-talk.

Are you being wrongly criticized? Instead of grumbling about how unfair life can be, tell yourself, "I care very little if I am judged by you." The more you repeat it, the less you will care about the judgment of another.

Do you find yourself being judgmental of others? Again and again say, "I do not even judge myself." Before long it will be true.

Are you angry because you've been blamed for something you didn't do? Repeat "My conscience is clear" until it really is.

Are you too much of a perfectionist? Too critical of yourself? Tell yourself, "It is the Lord who judges me."

What you tell yourself strongly influences what you become. In his book to the Christians at Philippi, Saint Paul wrote, "Whatever things are true, whatever things are noble, whatever things are just, whatever things are pure, whatever things are lovely, whatever things are of good report, if there is any virtue and if there is anything praiseworthy—meditate on these things" (Phil. 4:8).

What wonderful advice for your self-talk!

Step Four: Set Goals Today to Prepare for Tomorrow

"Lorraine and I went to a restaurant, and the young couple next to us bowed and prayed before they ate," Dick Meier recalls. "The fellow had shoulder-length hair and a shaggy beard. I whispered to Lorraine, 'How could someone who looks like him be talking to the same God I talk to?' On the way home from the restaurant, a car cut us off in traffic. The driver had short, nicely combed hair and was wearing a suit and tie—my kind of guy. On the back of his car was a bumper sticker that read: 'Jesus Is the Way.' Right then and there the Holy Spirit started working on me in the area of judging others."

When the Holy Spirit brings areas to your mind that need attention, what do you do? Most of us feel guilty for awhile, then we quickly forget and go right back to business as usual. But each of us should be aiming toward being better, more complete Christians tomorrow than we are today. To do this, we need to pick up on those areas that need work and do something about them. We need to set goals for ourselves, and we need to act on them. Perhaps the following action plan will help you make those positive changes.

Action Plan

1. Define just exactly what it is you want to change. (Be as specific as possible.)

   _____

   _____

   _____

   _____

2. List alternative solutions. (Write down any that occur to you—good, bad, or silly.)

   a. _____

   b. _____

   c. _____

   d. _____

3. Evaluate your solution ideas. Which are viable possibilities and which are not?

   a. _____

   b. _____

   c. _____

   d. _____

4. Write out your plan of attack:
   Action step one:

   _____

   _____

   _____

   _____

Action step two:

_____

_____

_____

_____

Action step three:

_____

_____

_____

_____

5. Get busy and implement your plan!

6. After you have given yourself some time to implement your action plan, pause and appraise your progress. List the steps you have taken and the progress you have made. Then decide on some meaningful rewards for yourself—you deserve it!

Action Steps	*Positive Progress*	*Rewards*
1.		
2.		
3.		
4.		
5.		

A whole and healthy pastor, fit for the work of God— that's the best gift you could possibly give your congregation. That's your responsibility to the church. In the next chapter, we will discuss the church's responsibility to you.

13

The Church's Responsibility

"My first church . . . ," Dick Meier says with a smile of remembrance. "We started it in a new section of Omaha, Nebraska—a truck driver and his family and me. That man had some wonderful, aggressive teenagers. His son led every single fellow on his high school football team to Christ! They had teen meetings on Thursday nights, and I, a college student, came and spoke to them. Later on I was asked to come more regularly. Then we invited all the moms and dads of the teenagers to meet with us in the truck driver's living room. That's how the church started.

"As the little group began to grow, the truck driver said to me, 'My rig earns enough for both you and my family. What about me giving you fifty dollars a week to pastor us while you're still in Bible college?' I accepted the offer, and we bought a home to use as a church. Later on, the house became the parsonage, and we built a nice new sanctuary next door."

All over the country, more new churches are now being formed than ever before. And because they are places where needs are being met and where people can worship God in honesty and sincerity, Bible-believing churches are growing faster than ever.

When things are going well, it's easy for pastor and

church to work together. But when there are difficulties, too many pastors tend to see their churches as their adversaries. It's too bad, because so often what the church really wants is to understand and to help.

We've talked at great length about a pastor's responsibility to the church. But what about the church? Where does its responsibility to the pastor fit in?

Certainly, church and pastor are intimately intertwined. The responsibility of each to the other requires that, to the best of their ability, they work together in harmony for the furthering of the Lord's work. We've already talked about the part you, the pastor, play in this partnership. Now let's look at the responsibilities of the church and specific ways a pastor can help his church meet them.

Communicate with the Pastor

Congregations consider themselves church families, and most truly do care about their pastors. Example after example in this book demonstrate how deeply people and churches care. Men and women of faith recognize the fact that the church in general, and their pastor in particular, occupy a crucial place in their lives. Because they care so much, members of the congregation want to communicate with their pastor. Trouble is, they don't always know how to do it effectively.

Too often when congregations either praise their pastor or correct him, they do it with an attitude that allows their lofty expectations to come crashing through. That makes it hard for the minister to hear the praise or accept the correction. If the expectations of the church are too high, it's up to the pastor to tell them so.

It is a common belief that great preachers make great churches. So if the church doesn't meet everyone's definition of greatness, what does that indicate? Right. It's the preacher's fault. But the actual fact is that it is great *churches* that make great *preachers*. Furthermore, greatness is demonstrated by the love the people in a congregation have for each other and for those God positions at their head as ministers. If your church is falling short, don't be too quick to accept it as your fault. Instead, talk to the congregation about working together on the shortcomings.

To open the lines of communication, a pastor can do two things: He can work with the governing body of the church, and he can enlist the help of the congregation as a whole. With the board of deacons or elders, emphasize your willingness to listen, your openness to new ideas, your desire to be objective. With you as a model, your board will likely treat you the same way. With the congregation, rather than speaking in generalities, give them specific examples and guidelines to help them see how they can implement true give-and-take communication in their own lives. Instead of saying, "Husbands, love your wives," let men know that sharing household chores is a practical way of demonstrating their love. Instead of saying, "Open the lines of communication," illustrate methods of nonthreatening sharing and active listening.

If you first learn to communicate with each other, every other step will be considerably easier.

Encourage the Pastor

Every pastor wants to have a successful ministry. When they look over at the great megachurches, some pastors find them encouraging—but others say just the opposite. To pastors who see all Christian ministers in equal partnership with God, it is wonderfully exciting to see how God is working in the church universal. But to those who equate numbers with success, it is devastating. "What's wrong with me?" they ask. "We have the same God. Why don't I see the same results?"

Pastors, please let us encourage you in the concept of being faithful. Different churches are at different stages of their lives. For some, it is a time to sow; for others it is a time to nurture. For still others, it is a time to reap. Too many churches measure their church against another church, their pastor against another pastor. It isn't fair. Any minister should only be measured against his own potential, the circumstances of the area in which his ministry is located, and his faithfulness to God. To do the best you can is to be successful.

Want to know how Jesus feels about the matter? He tells us in Matthew 25:14–30, in the story of the talents. Both the man who was given five talents and the one who was given two doubled their investment. Although one ended up with ten talents and the other with just four, both men received the same reward: "Well done, good and faithful servant." The master did not measure them against each other. The one who the master rebuked was the one who didn't even try.

Does your church encourage you? Does your congregation build you up? If so, respond in kind. If not, lead them into it by modeling the power of encouragement and praise. Be free with your own positive words any time you can do it sincerely. Praise and encourage and build others up both in private and from the pulpit. And whenever encouragement comes your way, express your appreciation for it. Let it be known that affirmation builds you up and helps you do your best.

Uphold Their End of the Ministry

"You're the pastor. That's your job. It's what we pay you for." Have you ever heard this response to your request for help in the ministry? Too often churches believe that the ministry is the sole responsibility of the pastor. It's up to you to help them understand that you are all in the ministry together.

To assist you in the ministry, your church has the responsibility to

- pay you a fair salary.

- not intrude unfairly on your time with your family.

- support you in prayer.

- accept you as their leader.

- do their part in the actual work of the ministry.

- cooperate in setting goals for the future.

You can help your congregation understand where your church is and how to set goals for where it will be going by examining the following questions together:

- What kind of congregation are we right now?

- What is our mission in this community?

- What are our strengths?

- What are our weaknesses?

- Do we have any special problems?

- In what areas have we developed in the last five years?

- Where do we want to be five years from now?

- Why do people come to our church?

- Why do they leave?

- What special projects should we take on?

Partners in the ministry, that's what you and your church are. If you help your congregation understand this, you will be helping yourself. Even more, you will be allowing your church family to personally experience the joy and blessing of serving the Lord.

Support the Integrity of the Ministry

"Two pastors were admitted to the hospital at about the same time," Dr. Paul Meier recalls. "One had serious problems—he had broken with reality, insisting he was a senator from the state of Texas. He was responding surprisingly well to treatment when, two days later, two board members from his church came and pulled him out of treatment. They explained that their church felt it was wrong for a pastor to be in a psychiatric hospital. The last I heard, that poor pastor was still psychotic, probably for life.

"The other pastor was suffering from a severe manic episode. No sooner was he admitted to the hospital than he insisted on making hospital rounds. He thought he was me. This pastor had been brought in by a couple of men from the church. 'He has problems,' they told me, 'but he's our pastor and we want to stand beside him.' His room was flooded with cards and letters and flowers from people in his church. After treatment with medication, this pastor returned to reality and to his church. For many years he continued in a thriving ministry."

The church has a responsibility to uphold the integrity of all aspects of the ministry. Here again you can teach by example. What is your attitude toward church members who have special problems or who need psychiatric care? How about those who have stumbled morally? Do you actively work toward restoration? Do you teach forgiveness? Do you model it before your people?

Members of the congregation, more than anyone else, can give you the support and encouragement you need. Let them know how much you need them.

Adapting to Changing Conditions

"I've finally changed my idea of what makes a person spiritual," Dick Meier says. "There was a time when I thought if I kept my church busy every night of the week, I'd keep them spiritual. It took awhile, but I finally learned: they, like me, need to limit their involvement."

As we approach the turn of the century, the church needs to take a look at its old time schedule. The Sunday morning service will stick; maybe there will be an evening service as well, but maybe not. Instead of a midweek service, churches will likely hold small group Bible studies where particular needs are addressed and met (such as handling divorce, alcoholism, financial problems, marriage difficulties, or learning healthy methods of parenting). In a small group setting, they will have the benefit of personal involvement, support, and fellowship.

Assuredly, many things will likely be going on in the church of tomorrow, but everyone won't be expected to be there for everything. More and more, people will be encouraged to pick and choose. Attendance just for the sake of attendance will no longer be considered a mark of spirituality.

In the years to come, people are likely to be more and more open to sharing hurts and discouragements as well as their blessings, successes, and wonderful answers to prayer. We will see more and more pastors who are able to relate to people right where they are. Rather than serving from up atop a pedestal, the attitude will be: "Folks, I'm here on this journey with you. I'm struggling too, so let's struggle together." It will be a good and healthy change for both the church and the pastor.

More churches will be pulling in church administrators who will be taking the business pressures off pastors. More churches will have extra staff members to lift some of the burden off the minister.

In the future, people will be less and less involved in the church. They will become more detached. This seems a certainty because people's lives are busier, and for most people, the church is no longer the center of social activity. In addition, people will have even more stresses on their lives. We are already seeing the mentality that people come to church to get, not to give. This will pose a special problem for pastors who do not have extra staff members.

As these changes take place, Pastor, take care to work together with the elders or deacons and begin to talk with them about what is needed in your church. Work with them on redefining the goals of the church as a whole and of your ministry in particular. Discuss where you together, by the grace of God, will be going, then pray from that standpoint. Encourage your congregation to determine to what degree they are willing to change to help accomplish those goals (an exercise that is sure to help you too). As the church shoulders more of its share of the responsibility for the ministry, the people will appreciate you more than ever.

To be a minister who faithfully leads his congregation in honor and service to God—this is the highest goal you can set for yourself. And, as a pastor, it is the best gift you can give your people.

14

Appreciation for the Front Line

Y
ou, dear Pastor, are vital to every one of us in the
Christian community. For some reason—perhaps
because we are human too—we are quicker to criticize you for what you aren't than to thank you for what you
are. It's unfortunate and unfair, because you deserve so
many heartfelt thank-yous. Let us take this opportunity to
express some of them.

Thank You for Your Flexibility

"When I was a young pastor in my first church, I was
never home," Dick Meier says. "We were starting that
church from scratch, so I spent my time knocking on doors,
trying to meet the quota I had set for myself. One day my
brother startled me by asking, 'When are you going to get
back into the Lord's will?' I said, 'What do you mean? I'm
out to save the world!' He said, 'That's your problem. Your
family needs you too.'

"I was shocked. My orientation was, 'If the Lord comes
back tonight, I want Him to find me faithfully serving Him,
not playing Tinkertoys with my kids.'" Under his brother's
loving but persistent chiding, Dick finally stepped back

and took a more realistic look at himself. He wasn't pleased with what he saw. "It was very hard," he says, "but I did change my ways."

It's tough to be flexible. And even when we do see problems, it's hard for us to change our approach to life.

"A nationally known pastor was sending out a lot of negative literature about me and our clinic," says Dr. Frank Minirth. "He'd never talked to me personally, but he was really angry. Although I'd never met the man, I had always respected him, so it really hurt to hear all that criticism. Paul Meier and I went to visit him and he said, 'Let me read you something.' It was his next newsletter, hot off the press and ready to go out. The man hotly berated psychiatrists and psychologists, just ran them up one side and down the other.

"Now, I knew enough about this pastor to know he had a good heart. He was just misinformed. When he finished reading us the article, Paul said, 'Good article. I could sign it myself.' You see, the main thrust was not putting down psychiatrists and psychologists, it was encouraging people to put Christ first in their lives. We agreed with that.

"'With us it's never psychiatry first,' we explained. 'It's always Christ first.'" The pastor considered this for quite some time. Then he said, 'I see you boys are all right. I'm still not too sure about that psychiatry stuff, but you're all right.'

"There were no more attacks from him. He had seen our hearts, discovered he was wrong about us, and he changed his mind."

Thank you, Pastor, for making changes even though it's so hard to do. In making the effort to change, you are teaching us to be more flexible.

Thank You for Caring for Yourself

More and more pastors are taking care to keep themselves in good physical shape. More are investing the time to keep spiritually healthy. And increasingly they are considering their emotional condition. Pastors are making the effort to talk to and share with other people. Even though they realize there is risk in doing so, they are willingly making themselves more vulnerable to their congregations.

Thank you, Pastor, for caring for yourself. In doing so, you are caring for us as well. And you are teaching us the importance of staying healthy—physically, spiritually, and emotionally.

Thank You for Needing Us

When we see ministers trying to do it all, we often ask them, "Do you think Jesus could have done a better job than His disciples did? Could He have worked more effectively with men and women? Could He have taught them better? Could He have healed more sick people?"

They always answer, "Well, of course He could! I mean, look at the resources Jesus had to work from."

So why didn't Jesus just do it? Why did He even bother with the disciples? One reason was undoubtedly for the purpose of modeling—He set the example of getting away. But another reason is that He wanted to prepare others to take over His ministry when He was gone. He wanted to give them time to be involved and to grow.

We appreciate the fact that you don't want a job done in a haphazard way. We know that if you did the job it would be done right. But we thank you for not depriving the rest of us of the chance to grow and develop in our Christian lives. And we appreciate you for refusing to exhaust yourself to where you burnout.

The Scripture tells of a time when Joshua was fighting the Amalekites. Moses was up on a hill, reaching his hands to heaven. As long as Moses' hands were up, Joshua was successful in the battle; but the moment his arms came down, the Amalekites prevailed. The problem was that Moses was getting more and more tired. When Moses could hold up his arms no longer, Aaron and another man came on either side of him and held his arms high (see Ex. 17:8–13).

What a beautiful picture of us needing each other! Sometimes we have to have support from each other or we just can't make it.

Thank you, Pastor, for needing us. Thank you for not being able to do it all alone.

Thank You for Your Success

Every pastor wants a successful ministry. But what is success? Is it big bucks? Is it fame? Is it a prestigious church bursting at the seams with people? Is it having your own show on radio? Or being an important television personality?

According to the world's standards, that is success. It's the business kind of success—numbers, money, fame. But let's back up a minute. The people in the Bible who were successful in God's eyes were people "after His own heart." It mattered not whether they did a little job or a large job. Take David for instance. He spent fifteen years running and hiding from Saul, and all that time he did little but survive and encourage the men around him. So what, then, is success? It is being the person God wants you to be in the place He wants you to be.

Pastor Jerry Root recalls, "In seminary we'd sit around and look at our classmates and say things like, 'Steve is going to be the next Billy Graham' or 'Paul is going to be the next Chuck Swindoll.' No one ever said, 'Look at old Vern. He's going to pastor three tiny churches out in the sticks thirty miles apart.' No, we had this idealized view. Now, years later, you look at the guys who went out thinking they were Billy Grahams and Chuck Swindolls. Those fellows haven't been very successful in their ministries because they started out expecting to be just like the big stars. They want to be famous for Jesus rather than to be servants of the Lord."

It is this that makes the church different from the world—we know what success really is. David Livingstone, that great missionary to Africa, never read business reports. He just had such a compassion for the souls and lives of the African people that he gave his whole life to serving them as a medical missionary. Sure it was inconvenient, but then the cross was inconvenient too.

Thank you, Pastor, for teaching us the difference between success and failure. Thank you for demonstrating that success is a matter of maximizing our own potential in a given situation, of doing the best we can today. Thank you for helping us understand that only one guy in the world can be the best at any given thing, and that even though none of us is likely to be that guy, we can do our best today.

Thank You for Being Faithful

By all external indications, King Solomon was wildly successful, much more so than the prophet Jeremiah, who was thrown into a cistern where he spent his time up to his armpits in slime. But which one would you rather be? Solomon, in his halfhearted devotion to God, or Jeremiah, who remained utterly faithful despite the fact that almost no one responded to his message?

Thank you, Pastor, for clinging to Jeremiah's kind of faithfulness. Thank you for being concerned about the world and the social issues facing us. Thank you for not being narrower than the Scriptures are narrow or broader than they are broad. Thank you for being faithful to your conscience and for being willing to speak out on those things that are important to you. Thank you for staying faithful to what God's Word says. Thank you for responding to your call to faithfulness.

Thank You for Being Willing to Serve

Joe Bayley, past president of David C. Cook Publishers, was a man who had a broad public ministry. At his funeral, a custodian stood up and said, "I want to say a word about Mr. Bayley. When he first came to David C. Cook, he saw me cleaning in the bathroom. I said 'Good morning, Mr. Bayley,' and he said, 'Sir, you always call me Joe.' Now that he's gone I'm going to call him Mr. Bayley."

Like Mr. Bayley, pastors get involved in the lives of people. Not everyone is as grateful as the custodian was. And most of the time your good and kind deeds, your generosities and gentle responses will never be known by anyone but the one humble soul to whom they were spoken. Many times you are called upon to serve people who repay you by draining you dry and using you to the point of exhaustion.

It's easy to love the lovely, but it can be so very hard to love the unlovely. Yet that's exactly what God calls us to do—to love those for whom love does not come easily.

Thank you, Pastor, for loving the unlovely. Thank you for

remembering that the King of kings himself is a servant. Thank you for being willing to be the servant to us all. Thank you for modeling Christian servanthood before the rest of us.

Thank You for Keeping Your Standards High

The poll conducted by *Christianity Today* and the Gallup organization indicated that fully half of the clergy surveyed felt they lived up to their own moral and ethical standards most of the time. About one in three admitted that while they tried to live up to their standards, they found it difficult. Only a very few felt their standards were impossible to maintain.

Thank you, Pastor, for keeping your standards high. Thank you for taking charge of your negative traits and tendencies, for keeping them under control, and for determining that discipline will rule your life. Thank you for not giving in to the easy way out. Thank you for encouraging us, by your words and your life, to set our own standards high and to constantly strive to live up to them.

Thank You for Your Hard Work

Confucius said, "Don't do to somebody else what you wouldn't want them to do to you." Not bad advice. At first it sounds very much like Jesus' words: "Do unto others what you would have them do unto you." But there is a very big difference. You could strictly adhere to Confucius' words without ever having to do anything at all. Not so with the words of Jesus. You cannot follow His teachings without rolling up your sleeves and getting to work.

Thank you, Pastor, for not settling for doing nothing.

Thank you for determining that for you, it's vital to actively "do unto others." Thank you for working tirelessly and asking so little in return. Thank you for encouraging us to do the same.

Thank You for Teaching Us from Your Experience

One of the most exciting things we have seen here at the clinic is that after pastors have come to us for treatment they almost always go back and share their experience with the church. And almost every church responds with love and acceptance. Pastors who cover up and are defensive, those who place themselves in the position of high confidant to God, men who never make mistakes, are headed for trouble.

It has been said that in every church there is a Judas and a Jezebel, just as there was a Judas for Jesus and a Jezebel for Elijah. Maybe so, but it is the Judases and the Jezebels who do the most to keep a pastor from getting overly confident.

We don't want you to have troubles, but when you do, we want you to know that we learn from them. We, too, grow through your rough times.

Thank you, Pastor, for teaching us from your experiences—even the painful ones. Thank you for allowing your personal Judas and Jezebel to prevent you from becoming overly confident.

Thank You for Hanging in There

The media would have us believe that pastors around the country are leaving their ministries in droves. But according to the *Christianity Today*-Gallup poll, only about three clergy members in ten indicated they "often" or "occasionally" considered leaving the ministry. Many responded that they have "never" considered dropping out.

When we weigh the pros of the life of a pastor against the cons, we sometimes wonder why you are willing to stay and shepherd us. Thank you, Pastor, for not bailing out when the going gets rough. Thank you for caring enough about us to hang in there. Thank you for showing us what it means to be truly tenacious and steadfast.

Thank You for Preparing for the Future

Many people claim that the 1990s and into the turn of the century is going to be a difficult period for the church. Certainly, we are seeing more needs demonstrated around us.

Things are changing in our churches, and churches need to be preparing and training helpers now for what will come tomorrow. While social issues should not take the place of spiritual issues, they, too, are part of the Christian life—and an important part at that.

Thank you, Pastor, for responding to the changing needs of the church. Thank you for seeking to balance your spiritual responsibilities and your concern for people's physical and emotional needs. Thank you for taking practical steps to meet the needs among us, just as Christ told us to.

Therefore we also pray always for you that our God would count you worthy of this calling, and fulfill all the good pleasure of His goodness and the work of faith with power, that the name of our Lord Jesus Christ may be glorified in you, and you in Him, according to the grace of our God and the Lord Jesus Christ (2 Thess. 1:11–12).

Notes

Chapter 1
1. Hank Wittemore, "Ministers Under Stress," *Parade Magazine*, 14 April 1991, 4.
2. Wittemore, "Ministers Under Stress," 4.
3. Wittemore, "Ministers Under Stress," 4.
4. Haddon Robinson, "A Profile of the American Clergyman," *Christianity Today*, 23 May 1980, 28.
5. Dr. David Congo & Jan Congo, *Less Stress: The 10-minute Stress Reduction Plan* (Ventura, CA: Regal Books, 1985).

Chapter 2
1. Haddon Robinson, "A Profile of the American Clergyman," *Christianity Today*, 23 May 1980, 27.
2. Minirth-Meier tapes are available from Dallas Christian Videos, 1–800-231-0095 or (214) 644-1905.

Chapter 3
1. Dr. David Congo & Jan Congo, *Less Stress: The 10-minute Stress Reduction Plan* (Ventura, CA: Regal Books, 1985).

Chapter 4
1. Marc Eisenson, *The Banker's Secret* (New York, N.Y.: Villard Books, 1990), 3.

Chapter 5
1. Peter Rutter, M.D., "Sex in the Forbidden Zone," *Psychology Today*, October 1989, 37.

Chapter 6
1. Bonnie Shipley Rice, "Married to the Man and the Ministry," *Leadership*, 1991, 68–69.
2. Rice, "Married to the Man and the Ministry," 70.
3. Rice, "Married to the Man and the Ministry," 73.

4. Rice, "Married to the Man and the Ministry," 73.
5. Rice, "Married to the Man and the Ministry," 69–72.
6. Rice, "Married to the Man and the Ministry," 73.
7. Rice, "Married to the Man and the Ministry," 71.

Chapter 9
1. Haddon Robinson, "A Profile of the American Clergy," *Christianity Today*, 23 May 1980.
2. Robinson, "A Profile of the American Clergy."

Chapter 10
1. *Christianity Today*, 19 August 1991, 44.

Chapter 11
1. Dr. David Congo & Jan Congo, *Less Stress: The 10-minute Stress Reduction Plan* (Ventura, CA: Regal Books, 1985).
2. Herbert J. Freudenberger, *Burnout: The High Cost of High Achievement* (New York, N.Y.: Doubleday and Co., 1980), 11–12.

About the Authors

Together, the authors of *What They Didn't Teach You in Seminary* have more than thirty-three years of experience in the pastorate.

Dr. Richard Meier served as a pastor for twenty-three years before joining the Minirth-Meier Clinic in Richardson, Texas, as a counselor. He received the D.Min. from Trinity Theological Seminary in Newburg, Indiana; his Th.M. from Clarksville School of Theology in Clarksville, Tennessee; and his M.A. in counseling from Liberty University in Lynchburg, Virginia.

Paul Meier, M.D., co-founder of the Minirth-Meier Clinics, has an M.A. from Dallas Theological Seminary and has taught pastoral counseling in seminary. He received his M.D. from the University of Arkansas College of Medicine.

Frank Minirth, M.D., co-founder of the Minirth-Meier Clinics, also has an M.A. in theology from Dallas Theological Seminary and is an associate professor of ministries at the seminary. Dr. Minirth received his M.D. from the University of Arkansas.

Dr. Brian Newman served as a pastor while studying to receive his M.A. in biblical counseling from Grace Theological Seminary and holds a certificate in biblical studies from Grace. Dr. Newman received his D.Phil. from Oxford Graduate School and is director of Inpatient Services at the Minirth-Meier Clinic in Richardson, Texas.

Dr. David Congo had seven years of pastoral experience

before studying to receive his Ph.D. in clinical psychology from the Rosemead School of Psychology. He is now a practicing psychologist with the Minirth-Meier-Stoop Clinic in Laguna Hills, California.

Dr. Allen Doran has an M.A. in theology from Denver Seminary and his M.D. in psychiatry from the University of Texas Medical School at Houston. A board-certified psychiatrist, Dr. Doran completed his residency in psychiatry at Harvard Medical School and is the medical director of Canyon Springs Hospital and a counselor with the Minirth-Meier Clinic in Roseville, California.

For general information about other Minirth-Meier Clinic branch offices, counseling services, educational resources and hospital programs, call toll free 1-800-545-1819. National Headquarters: (214) 669-1733 (800) 229-3000.